Moulton
College

NORTHAMPTONSHIRE

Profit through Skill

ALPINE
GARDENING

ALPINE
GARDENING

CHRIS & VALERIE WHEELER

GUILD OF MASTER CRAFTSMAN PUBLICATIONS

First published 2002 by
Guild of Master Craftsman Publications Ltd
Castle Place, 166 High Street,
Lewes, East Sussex BN7 1XU

ISBN 1 86108 300 9

A catalogue record for this book is available from the
British Library.

Editor: David Arscott
Book and cover design: Fineline Studios

Set in Centaur

Colour origination by Viscan Graphics (Singapore)
Printed and bound by Kyodo Printing (Singapore) under the
supervision of MRM Graphics, Winslow, Buckinghamshire, UK

CONTENTS

Introduction	I	

Chapter 1	What is an alpine?	3

Chapter 2	Designing with alpines	15

Chapter 3	Cultivation	31
	Position	31
	Soils	32
	Planting	32
	Watering and feeding	34
	Pruning and trimming	34
	Problems, pests and diseases	36

Chapter 4	Propagation	41
	Seeds	41
	Cuttings	46
	Division	50

Chapter 5	Raised beds (including peat beds)	53
	Building a raised bed	54
	Filling a raised bed	57
	Maintenance	59

Chapter 6	Troughs and other containers	67
	Sinks and troughs	67
	Some other containers	74

Chapter 7	Other ways of growing alpines	83
	Gravel areas	83
	Around ponds	86
	Paving and patios	87
	Walls	90
	Borders	90

Chapter 8	Plant descriptions	98

Acknowledgements	139	
About the authors	140	
Index	141	

INTRODUCTION

The numerous ideas in this book aim to encourage those of you daunted by the very word 'alpine'. Convinced that alpines have to be grown on rock gardens, many people don't even try to grow them, ignoring them altogether or merely admiring them from a distance. There are, however, so many ways to display alpines other than in rock gardens – a fact of great importance if your space is limited. We would like to encourage you to discover these appealing plants and to be inspired by some of the suggestions within these pages. Everyone should be able to enjoy growing alpines, and we hope to give you the confidence to do so.

Their appeal is due above all to their diminutive size and the fact that a large variety can be fitted into a small space. They often produce prolific flowers in clear bright colours over neat tidy mounds or tufts of foliage. There is a huge range of hardy alpines suitable for every garden, and we include a section giving detailed descriptions of those mentioned throughout the text.

Inspiring plans for some of the features will give you ideas to get started, while step-by-step sequences of planting and propagation should be of great help and encouragement, especially to beginners. The photographs illustrate individual alpines, planting associations and alpine features.

WHAT IS AN ALPINE?

This book is concerned with the hardy alpines and rock plants that will thrive happily outside all year in suitable positions in the garden, rather than those that require more specialized treatment in an alpine house or frame.

Definition of an alpine

The term 'alpine' is used to describe small, low-growing plants that originate from a wide range of habitats, not just from alpine regions. The cultivation of these plants can be an absorbing hobby and a lifelong interest, with the possibility of collecting and growing together alpines from many parts of the world. They are very adaptable, as many species originate from similar environments, even though they may come from different regions of the world.

Left **An area of garden full of alpines from many parts of the world**

Alpines, in the strictest sense, are plants that grow at high altitudes in alpine regions, although even these cover a variety of conditions. Adapted specifically to deal with a harsh environment, such as hot days, freezing temperatures at night, snow and strong, biting winds, these plants can be more demanding to grow in cultivation. In the wild, they often grow lodged in rock crevices and cracks, or in screes formed by a massed collection of stones, and they have long roots to reach water and nutrients deep down. They are by necessity more

In their natural habitat, alpines are covered by snow for much of the winter – in cultivation, this snow covering rarely lasts long

specialized to cope with their demanding environment, and do not always respond readily to garden cultivation, as it can be very difficult to emulate the right conditions. Constant moisture at the roots in winter is a particular problem few high alpines can tolerate, as they are used to very free drainage. In the wild they are surrounded by constantly moving fresh air, which means that warm, humid summers do not suit them either. They tend to have a short growing season, as they grow and flower in their natural habitat when the snow retreats.

Examples of plants and their habitat

Silene acaulis is widely distributed in the Northern Hemisphere, being found in gritty conditions with plenty of moisture at the roots during the growing season, but drier at other times. It flowers freely in the wild, but far less so in cultivation, though it grows well enough in gritty, poor soil.

Soldanella species are found in the European Alps on high alpine meadows, and start to flower as soon as the snow begins to melt. In the garden, they need to grow in humus-rich yet gritty soil in a cool position. In their native habitat, the snow covering protects the emerging buds, whereas in the garden these will be exposed and may be killed by prolonged cold.

In a more general sense, alpines and rock plants include a whole range of small plants from a variety of habitats, and not just mountainous regions. The less harsh conditions below the tree line, and down into the high pastures, woods and meadows, mean that these plants are more amenable to growing in our gardens. Their natural conditions are easier to create, and they have a longer growing and flowering season.

In the high pastures can be found genera such

as *Saponaria*, *Gentiana*, *Campanula* and *Helianthemum*, all requiring free drainage but plenty of water during the growing season. For example, *Gentiana acaulis* is found in the European Alps, where it grows in the high meadows among rocks and grasses.

Woodland plants, on the other hand, like cool, damp but still well-drained soil and partial shade. *Anemone nemerosa* is found in woodland and mountain pastures in Europe and Britain, and grows happily in partially shaded, moist but not wet soil in the garden.

Plants commonly grown as alpines include:

* mountain plants that like brightly lit positions, similar to the high light intensity of their natural habitat
* woodland plants, preferring dappled shade similar to the wooded slopes
* shade-loving plants, used to north-facing crevices
* sun-loving plants from Mediterranean hillsides
* small plants from coastal habitats
* slow-growing small plants from other regions

Alpines can be deciduous or evergreen woody plants, or herbaceous perennials. There are very few annual alpines. Helianthemums, parahebes and *Penstemon pinifolius* are examples of woody evergreens, retaining their leaves all year round on a bushy, woody framework of branches. *Persicaria vaccinifolia* has a woody structure, with trailing stems, but the leaves fall in autumn, so it is a deciduous plant. Herbaceous perennial alpines include *Scutellaria* and *Veronica*, whose stems die back each year, producing new growth from the centre of the plant. One annual alpine worth growing is *Ionopsidium acaule*, simply because it is so pretty and easily grown from seed.

Extending the colour range

Many plants grown as alpines tolerate a wide range of conditions, although others require more care and more exacting conditions. There is a huge range of wild species, with all the appeal of wild flowers, as well as numerous cultivated hybrids that extend the colour ranges. Certain genera have been extensively hybridized, producing a far greater range of forms and colours than can be found in the wild. Helianthemums, for instance, have been bred with pastel and bright flower colours, larger or double flowers, and a range of leaf colours from grey to dark green. *Lewisia cotyledon* can now be found with blooms of magenta, deep pink, orange, yellow and pure white, derived by breeding from the wild species, which usually has pink-striped white or pink flowers. It is, however, naturally variable, with pure white, apricot and yellow forms being found in the wild, allowing for greater scope in breeding. New cultivars of *Saxifraga* are available in a vast array of flower colours, including more unusual shades such as salmon and apricot, as well as variations on the natural pink and yellow colours.

Magenta blooms on this *Lewisia cotyledon* **hybrid are the result of breeding to extend the colour range**

The mounded form of *Sedum spathulifolium*

Characteristics

Plant shapes and growth habits

There is a huge range of plant shapes and growth habits among alpines and rock plants.

Mounds or cushions

These have short stems, closely packed together and clothed in small or tiny leaves, creating a dense or more loosely arranged mound that tends to be slightly higher in the centre and curves gently down around the sides to the ground. Some are soft to the touch, while others can be very hard and dense.

Examples: *Draba, Minuartia, Thymus serpyllum* 'Elfin'.

Tufted

Shoots and leaves arise from the base of the plant in tufts, usually forming low, compact plants and slowly increasing clumps.

Examples: *Aster alpinus, Erinus alpinus, Phyteuma.*

Erinus alpinus **is a typical tufted alpine**

Veronica pectinata **has long, prostrate or trailing stems**

Prostrate

Stems grow horizontally along the ground, or may cascade or trail if grown in a wall or trough. Leaves may be close together, almost hiding the stem, or more widely spaced. Stems may be a different colour to the leaves, creating an attractive contrast.

Examples: *Thymus serpyllum, Saponaria ocymoides, Hypericum reptans, Gypsophila repens.*

Bushy

These have a shrubby nature, with stems becoming woody as they mature. They may be low growing, rounded or upright bushes.

Examples: *Thymus* × *citriodorus, Helianthemum, Hypericum olympicum, Origanum microphyllum*

Helianthemum 'Beechpark Red' **has a bushy habit**

Rosettes

Individual rosettes are composed of numerous leaves arranged around a central point, and plants may consist of a few or many rosettes. Some are clustered closely together, mounding themselves up into low domes, while others may form flatter mats. Leaf size and shape varies considerably in different rosette plants: those of *Lewisia cotyledon* are long and fleshy while many saxifrages have tiny, pointed or spoon-shaped leaves that can be very hard.

Examples: *Saxifraga, Sempervivum, Lewisia, Androsace.*

Foliage and flowers

The array of foliage and flowers in terms of colours and shapes adds to the beauty and interest of alpines, and the varying flowering seasons allow colour to be provided for much of the year with a suitable choice of plants.

The colour range among alpines is considerable, particularly when cultivated varieties are also taken into account. You can find alpines with flowers of white, greenish-white and cream; all shades of yellow from pale lemon to deep golden; all shades of pink from palest blush to deep rosy pink; magenta; a range of blues from powder blue to deep gentian blue; lilac, mauve and purple; and a few instances of red, orange and apricot.

Clustered rosettes of *Sempervivum tectorum* **'Nigrum'**

Small, rounded white flowers and spiky foliage of a saxifrage

Chiastophyllum oppositifolium **has long, pendant sprays of golden flowers and toothed, fleshy leaves**

The shapes of flowers, even on this miniature scale, have as much variety as those of larger plants. They may be rounded, bell-shaped, star-shaped, lipped or tubular, borne on individual stems or in clustered heads or spikes.

Although they are traditionally thought to be mostly spring- and early summer-flowering, alpines do have varying flowering seasons, with many blooming during the later part of the year. They can have just one short burst of flower or produce flowers over several weeks; they may have their main flush in spring, with a second flush in autumn; or they may produce flowers over a period of several months. There are even some alpines that seldom seem to be without a flower, particularly during mild winters, such as *Erodium × variabile* 'Bishop's Form'.

Leaf shape is infinitely variable: you will find linear, sword-shaped, oval, rounded, spiky, needle-like, palmate and trifoliate shapes, among others. You can find alpines with leaves in all shades of green, as well as golden, grey, silver, variegated and purple. Some alpines have red-tinted leaves, or they may take on autumn colours (*Persicaria, Geum*), or show deeper, brighter colours during hot, sunny summer weather (*Sedum oreganum*, some sempervivums).

The pink, starry blooms of *Sedum spurium* 'Variegatum' contrast with its variegated foliage

Hardiness

The hardiness of particular alpines and their tolerance of winter damp are important characteristics to consider when choosing which plants to grow in your garden. This will also depend on the region you live in, as some alpines will thrive in drier parts of the country; some will survive in milder areas but may suffer outside in cold regions; and others may prefer a moister atmosphere.

Types of plants to look for

that are likely to be particularly tolerant and hardy:

✳ Plants with leathery leaves – these are more resistant to moisture loss
✳ Evergreens
✳ Woody plants – these have a framework above ground, so are less susceptible to rotting off or to early slug damage

Types to avoid

include those with foliage that will trap moisture and may rot in winter or damp conditions:

✳ Excessively woolly foliage
✳ Leaves with a heavy meal or 'bloom'
✳ Very hairy leaves
✳ Very tight buns or rosettes of soft foliage

Very tight-domed alpines, and those with woolly, hairy or intensely silver leaves, often will not tolerate winter conditions outside – these ones are growing in an alpine house

Brief guide to growing conditions

We aim to defuse the myth of all alpines being difficult and needing to be cosseted or grown only on a rock garden. A wide range of habitats can be created in the garden without the need for a traditional rockery or rock garden. As long as you consider the requirements of the plants, matching their natural growing conditions as closely as you

Top dressing alpine plantings with grit helps to keep the necks of plants dry

can, you will be able to grow a vast range of alpines without much trouble. Even in a small garden, several different habitats can be created, either in troughs or small raised beds.

Probably the two most important factors to take into account are the amount of drainage that can be provided and the type of soil the plant will be growing in. The majority of alpines require well-drained conditions, particularly around the neck of the plant. Take into account your soil type, or the soil or compost you are providing or mixing yourself. Some alpines are tolerant of a wide range of soils, while others require either limy or acidic soil and will suffer adversely in the wrong kind.

Good drainage is conveniently achieved by growing alpines in soil raised above ground level – in raised beds and troughs, for example. Top dressing with sharp chippings or grit is an additional benefit, as this will keep the necks of the plants from becoming damp or lying in moist soil.

Many alpines will, however, happily grow in small borders or along the edges of borders, as long as the soil is well drained and does not lie wet during the winter.

Throughout this book we shall examine several possible ways of growing alpines, to encourage both beginners and more experienced gardeners to try out this wonderful range of small plants.

CHAPTER TWO

DESIGNING WITH ALPINES

Planting alpines in your garden requires the same care and attention to positioning as with larger plants, taking into account plant shape and growth habit, foliage and flower colour, and harmony or contrast with neighbouring plants. Whether you are exclusively using alpines or mixing them with other small plants, it is important to think about the overall effect of your planting.

It is possible to grow a large number of alpines in a restricted space because of their small size, and therefore a greater variety of plants can be enjoyed than if the same area were planted with shrubs or herbaceous perennials. They are ideal for the smaller gardens that many people have these days, but they can be equally valuable for features within larger gardens.

A small garden could have one or more raised beds filled with a variety of alpines and dwarf shrubs, with miniature bulbs adding colour in early spring. Troughs and pots of alpines could be added, giving a year-round display every bit as colourful and interesting as that of larger plants, with the advantage that a much greater range of plants can be grown. Even a tiny courtyard garden can hold a few pots of alpines, choosing those with attractive foliage as well as flowers for a longer season of interest.

Left **This raised bed contains sun-loving alpines, and provides a shady area for saxifrages beneath a dwarf** *Acer*

A larger garden may have one or more areas devoted to alpine plants, perhaps using troughs and pots on a gravel area that is also planted, or having a paved area with some raised beds. If the soil is well drained, beds and borders can also be used for alpine plantings.

Choosing alpines to grow together

You need to choose alpines that require similar conditions in order to grow them together. Because of their natural habitat, most prefer excellent drainage and a sunny open position. However, there are also many woodland and shade-loving plants, so these can be grown in a shady corner where they will not be subject to the heat and glare of the midday sun. In the winter, though, they will benefit from as much light as possible, so shade from deciduous shrubs or trees is preferable to that cast all year round by dense evergreens or solid fences.

Before planting an alpine, you need to consider whether it needs well-drained soil; extra sharp drainage in very gritty soil; moist, peaty soil; lime-free soil; sun or shade. Whether you are planning a raised bed in full sun, a peat bed in the shade or a trough outside your door that receives sun for half the day, you need to be sure that your plants will like those conditions.

Plants for different situations

To give you an idea, here are some examples of suitable alpines for a variety of different situations in the garden. In a sunny, sharply drained raised bed, choose *Anacyclus*, *Convolvulus lineatus*, *Dianthus*, *Erigeron compositus* var. *discoideus*, *Phlox*, *Pterocephalus perennis* and *Veronica prostrata*, which all thrive in these conditions. More diminutive alpines suitable for a sunny trough include *Alyssum spinosum* 'Roseum', *Asperula gussonei*, *Dianthus* 'Berlin Snow', *Limonium* and *Minuartia stellata*.

Plants such as *Acinos alpinus*, *Erinus*, *Papaver*, *Scutellaria* and *Sisyrinchium* would relish a hot gravel garden, where they have room to self-seed and form colonies or patches. Add sun-loving, bushy helianthemums and carpeting thymes that will also reward you with masses of flowers in this situation.

Anacyclus pyrethrum var. *depressus* **is ideal for a sharply drained raised bed**

Below Acinos alpinus **and** *Minuartia circassica* **growing in a hot gravel garden together with dwarf irises**

Geraniums, such as *Geranium sanguineum* var. *striatum*, have a long flowering season, producing a succession of flowers over many months

Arabis ferdinandi-coburgii 'Old Gold' has early flowers as well as variegated leaves

Alpines for a shadier position include *Chiastophyllum, Epilobium crassum, Lewisia* and *Viola*, as well as many of the saxifrages. These will tend to scorch in the heat of summer sun, so they need to be shaded at least during the hottest part of the day. However, they do require as much light as possible during winter. Plants such as *Aruncus* and *Dodecatheon* prefer a moist soil and will wilt in sun-baked positions. They will, however, thrive in a sunny position as long as their roots are in moist soil, even if the leaves wilt during the midday sun.

Seasons of interest

It is possible to select alpines with a variety of foliage and flowers, and even seed-heads, to give you colour and interest for much of the year. Some alpines, such as *Erodium, Geranium* and *Lewisia*, have particularly long flowering seasons, producing their blooms over many months. Others, including many campanulas and some veronicas and anemones, produce one flush and then another one later in

the year. Interesting or colourful foliage adds a lot to an alpine planting, even when flowers are finished. Think of the succulent rosettes of sempervivums, in many shades of green as well as red, grey-purple and mahogany. Some change colour with the seasons, becoming bronzed or a deeper red in summer, while others have differently

Right *Solidago multiradiata* **is valuable for its late summer and autumn flowers**

Below **The flowering buds of** *Saxifraga burseriana* **'Prince Hal' appear in mid to late winter**

coloured tips to the leaves. Many alpines have silvery leaves (*Achillea* 'Huteri', *Convolvulus lineatus*, *Origanum microphyllum*), while others are variegated (*Arabis ferdinandi-coburgii* 'Old Gold', *Aubrieta* 'Aureovariegata').

You may wish to limit your choice to alpines that flower at a particular time of year, perhaps planting a small raised bed or particular area with those which look colourful in spring or autumn. Phloxes, aubrieta and many primulas, for instance, have a single period of flowering, producing a mass of bloom in spring. On the other hand, *Solidago* and *Persicaria* bloom in autumn only, and the leaves of the latter also show red and bronze autumn colour before they fall. Some sedums also produce their starry flowers late in the season.

Plant shapes

Consider the habit and shape of plants that you put together, as this affects the overall appearance of the planting. Even among small alpines, there is such a wide range of plant shapes and habits that a combination can look interesting from this aspect alone. Bushy and shrubby alpines, such as helianthemums, some thymes and *Hypericum olympicum*, add height and woody structure. Tufted alpines have leaves growing from one or more centres at soil level, often forming slowly increasing clumps. *Aster alpinus*, *Anemone caroliniana*, *Dianthus*, *Scabiosa japonica* var. *alpina* and *Sisyrinchium* fall into this category. Alpines such as saxifrages and sempervivums grow as clusters of rosettes which themselves form low mats or mounds. Other mounded or cushion-forming alpines often form tight domes or mats of tiny, closely spaced leaves, which may be sharp and needle-like — sometimes forming a really hard cushion, sometimes being softer and more rounded. Some alpines grow as tight mats or more spreading carpets, with long stems clothed in leaves that cover the ground or can be allowed to trail over the sides of containers or walls.

This brief summary of the types of plant habit gives you some idea of the range available, and it is applicable to alpines of varying sizes.

Colours

There is a vast range of both foliage and flower colours among alpine plants, so it is possible to choose all sorts of combinations, just as you would with larger plants. You can have subtle or bright colours, harmonizing or contrasting colours, or one-colour schemes.

Use foliage to form a background or as a foil to flower colours. Choose attractive combinations to give you a long period of interest, especially when planning on a very small scale when every individual plant will be noticed. Remember to use

Sempervivums grow as clusters of rosettes, gradually forming a mound

The green and gold leaves of *Thymus* '**Doone Valley**' **harmonise with yellow** *Hypericum cerastioides* **and give contrast to** *Phlox subulata* '**Amazing Grace**'

the various shades of green, from yellow-green, fresh apple green, olive green, deep sombre green and blue-green, as all of these create an interesting backbone. Use golden and silvery foliage, reddish and bronze-tinted leaves, bearing in mind that the foliage of some alpines shows autumn colour before falling. Variegated leaves can add some bright colour as well, but be careful not to use too much together or the effect can be overpowering.

We have already discussed the range of flower colours in Chapter I, and the appeal of many alpines lies in their bright, clear flower colours. There are also many with more muted flower colours, however, so you have a huge choice. Hybrids of a range of popular alpines have been bred with brighter colours, such as red, orange and magenta, seldom seen in wild species, and these have added to the range available.

Blue- and yellow-flowered alpines always look attractive together, as do soft pink and mauve, dark purple and rosy pink, or purple and white. A group with cream, pale and deep blue, soft yellow and golden flowers makes a cheerful display, while a combination of blush pink, powder blue and pale lilac has a soft, muted appearance. Deep blue, gold and red flowers make a dazzling show, whereas lemon yellow, cream and white make a light, calm and restful group.

Of course, you can plant many different colours together, especially on a larger feature, but particular colour combinations, either in groups or in small features, do look attractive. Use foliage as well as flower colours when planning your groups. To help you with some ideas, we have selected a few groups of alpines based on the points discussed.

✳ Use deep blue *Veronica prostrata*, *Gentiana septemfida* or *Phyteuma scheuchzeri* together with lemon-yellow *Achillea* × *lewisii* 'King Edward' and golden *Helianthemum* 'Sterntaler'. Replace the *Achillea* with scarlet *Penstemon pinifolius* for a bright splash, and add further golden-flowering alpines such as *Hypericum olympicum* or *Ranunculus gramineus*. The addition of *Sedum oreganum* provides brilliant red, glossy, fleshy leaves as well as golden starry flowers.

Mauve *Campanula* 'Birch Hybrid' and pink *Antennaria microphylla* **look attractive together**

✳ The deep purple, star-shaped flowers and toothed, heart-shaped leaves of *Campanula poscharskyana* 'Stella' combine beautifully with the rock rose *Helianthemum* 'Ben Ledi', which has dark green narrow leaves and deep rose-red rounded flowers.

✳ A softly coloured group of neat, compact alpines for a trough or small raised bed includes *Dianthus* 'Whatfield Wisp', with faintly blush pink blooms, *Campanula cochleariifolia* 'Elizabeth Oliver', which has double hanging flowers of palest powder blue, and *Erigeron compositus* var. *discoideus*, with its pale lavender-rayed flowers.

✳ Use silver foliage to lighten a group, or to create a cool scheme with white-flowered alpines. *Origanum microphyllum* and *Stachys iva* are ideal for troughs and raised beds, while more spreading types such as *Tanacetum densum* subsp. *amani*, *Achillea* 'Huteri' and *Anthemis marschalliana* make lovely mounds on gravel areas or at the front of well-drained borders.

✳ An effective group of contrasting shapes could consist of the tufted, sword-like leaves of *Sisyrinchium idahoense*, the mats of needle-like leaves of *Minuartia circassica*, trailing *Gypsophila repens* 'Fratensis', the shrubby, spiky *Alyssum spinosum* 'Roseum' and the leathery rosettes of *Limonium bellidifolium*. The small, neat flowers of blue-mauve, white, pink and pinkish-mauve also enhance this group.

21

Small ferns are ideal for planting in partial shade with alpines such as *Saxifraga* 'Winifred Bevington'

Using alpines with other plants

Many other small plants can be incorporated with alpines, including miniature conifers and dwarf shrubs, small ferns and dwarf bulbs. The important point to remember is the scale of the plants you put together, so that they do not look incongruous next to one another. Make sure that any conifers and shrubs really are miniature or dwarf species, and not young specimens of larger plants labelled as dwarf. The best way of ensuring this is to purchase your plants from a reputable or specialist nursery (more of this later in the chapter).

Miniature shrubs and conifers can form a backbone or give additional structure to alpine plantings. Those that are evergreen provide useful foliage during winter, while flowering shrubs add further colour in spring or summer. Bushy and upright forms can add valuable height if required, while prostrate kinds can cover the ground or border edge or trail over the sides of sinks, troughs or raised beds. Small ferns are interesting to plant in suitable locations, from tiny ones that are ideal for troughs to small forms for partially shaded, moist peat beds. A whole range of dwarf bulbs is available to incorporate with alpines in any feature in the garden, adding colour in spring, summer or autumn, depending on the species. Choose bulbs of suitable heights and size of flower to mix with your alpines.

Bright orange flowers of the dwarf shrub
Berberis × *stenophylla* **'Corallina Compacta'** add
welcome colour to this alpine bed

Suggestions
for plants to use

Miniature conifers show a range of shapes and
foliage colour, adding structure and substance to
an alpine planting, and their evergreen nature is
valuable. Narrow, columnar forms such as *Juniperus
communis* 'Compressa' are useful to contrast with
mounded or prostrate alpines, and are attractive

when surrounded with carpeting thymes or
veronicas, for example. Bun-shaped conifers include
Chamaecyparis lawsoniana 'Gnome', with dark green,
tightly packed foliage; *Thuja occidentalis* 'Caespitosa',
with thread-like yellowish-green branches and
flattened foliage; and *Cryptomeria japonica*

'Compressa', a slow-growing green bush that becomes bronze during winter.

Suitable shrubs for troughs and raised beds include forms of *Ilex crenata*, *Salix* 'Boydii' and *S. serpyllifolia*, *Hebe* 'Colwall', *H. raoulii* var. *pentasepala* and *H.* 'Jasper', and *Ulmus parvifolia* 'Hokkaido'. Small, low-growing shrubs for gravel gardens and front of border include deciduous *Berberis thunbergii* cultivars such as 'Bagatelle' and 'Kobold', evergreen *Berberis* × *stenophylla* 'Corallina Compacta', and dwarf forms of *Daphne*, *Genista*, *Lavandula* and *Spiraea*. There are many small shrubs for peat beds, too, including slow-growing forms of *Rhododendron*, *Cassiope*, *Kalmiopsis* and *Phyllodoce*.

Suggested miniature ferns to use, growing up to 15cm (6in) in height, include *Woodsia polystichoides* and *Asplenium trichomanes* 'Incisum'. Those up to 30–40cm (12–16ins) include *Dryopteris erythrosora* 'Prolifera' and *Polystichum setiferum* 'Congestum'.

Use the tiniest bulbs you can find for sinks and troughs or pans of alpines. There are miniature narcissi, irises and tulips that grow only a few centimetres (or inches) in height, perfect for growing among compact, neat alpines. Those that reach 15–25cm (6–10in) in height can be planted among alpines in raised beds, gravel areas and pots, while those up to 40cm (16in) or so are suitable for putting at the front of a border or in a larger container among more robust alpines. You will come across many spring-flowering bulbs such as narcissi, tulips, irises, crocuses, scillas and puschkinias, but do seek out summer- and autumn-flowering types as well, in order to extend the season. For summer, choose bright blue *Allium beesianum* or pinkish-purple *Allium cernuum*. Autumn-flowering bulbs include *Leucojum* and *Allium callimischon* subsp. *haemostictum*. Dwarf cyclamen such as *Cyclamen hederifolium* and *C. coum* also add autumn and winter flowers.

Types of alpine to choose

If you have never grown alpines before, it makes sense to choose some of the easy, reliable growers to start with. Once you have gained some confidence with those, you will want to explore different varieties and more unusual types, and perhaps go on to grow more demanding alpines. If you try growing ones that need special care from the start, it is easy to become disillusioned when they fail to thrive.

Beginners' alpines

This is not an exhaustive list, but includes suggestions for attractive, reliable alpines to grow in particular situations. Full details of the plants can be found in Chapter 8.

Trough
Armeria juniperifolia, *Thymus serpyllum* 'Minimus', *Gypsophila repens* 'Fratensis', any of the named cultivars of *Phlox douglasii*, such as 'Crackerjack' (crimson-red), 'Rosea' (pale pink) or 'Violet Queen' (rich violet), *Dianthus* 'Whatfield Joy', *D.* 'La Bourboule' and *D.* 'Whatfield Wisp', *Sempervivum*.

Raised bed/gravel area
Achillea 'Huteri', *Campanula garganica*, *Dianthus* 'Dainty Dame', *Hypericum olympicum*, *Parahebe catarractae* 'Delight', *Penstemon pinifolius*, *Sedum spurium*, *Thymus pulegioides* 'Archer's Gold', *Veronica prostrata*.

Front of border
Achillea 'Huteri', *Geranium sanguineum*, *Helianthemum* 'Sterntaler' or *H.* 'Wisley Primrose', *Primula denticulata*, *Parahebe catarractae* or *P. lyallii*, *Sedum kamtschaticum* var. *floriferum* 'Weihenstephaner Gold', *Thymus* 'Porlock'.

Iris reticulata is an excellent dwarf, spring-flowering bulb for troughs or raised beds

Once you have mastered the easier alpines, you can progress to more unusual varieties, and by visiting specialist shows or nurseries you will find many exciting plants to try. You must expect to fail with some of them – we all do – but don't let that discourage you. Make sure you know the particular plant's requirements beforehand, by asking the nurseryman or a more experienced grower, or by looking up the details.

A display of sempervivums at a specialist alpine nursery

Alpines for more experienced gardeners

If you have grown alpines before, or are keen to progress to more demanding or unusual ones, then you have a huge choice. Many of these are equally reliable and sturdy, but may just need extra sharp drainage or a particular soil mix. Some are so small and dainty that complete beginners quail at the thought of keeping them alive.

Troughs

Asperula gussonei, Alyssum serpyllifolium, Campanula cochleariifolia 'Elizabeth Oliver', *Dianthus* 'Berlin Snow', *Minuartia stellata, Silene acaulis.*

Raised bed/gravel area

Anacyclus pyrethrum var. *depressus, Convolvulus lineatus, Erodium* × *variabile* 'Bishop's Form', *Gentiana acaulis* or *G. septemfida, Pterocephalus perennis, Sisyrinchium macrocarpon.*

Peat bed

Autumn-flowering gentians, *Calceolaria* 'John Innes', *Soldanella, Lithodora diffusa.*

Sources of alpine plants

Alpines are available from a number of different outlets, but beware of buying them from places that have no experienced staff to advise you, or from market stalls or shops, unless you are sure of what the plant is. Not all plants labelled as alpines are slow-growing and compact, and you need to know what their growth habit is, their spread and their suitability for where you are planting them.

Specialist nurseries and plant centres

There are many nurseries that specialize in alpines, and some plant centres have reputable alpine departments. Visit any that you can get to, making sure that you know their opening hours beforehand. The proprietors and/or their staff are usually only too happy to help and advise on selection, so don't be afraid to ask, particularly if you are a beginner. The advantage of visiting is that you can see what the alpines look like, and sometimes see mature specimens growing in a display garden. Many specialist nurseries are run by the owners, and may be quite small, but they grow their plants themselves and have a vast fund of knowledge about them. They will be able to advise on the best plants for particular situations, tell you whether any plant is especially difficult or challenging, and give you advice on many other aspects.

You can also buy alpines by mail order and, indeed, some nurseries will only deal in this way. You will find advertisements in all the good gardening magazines, so send off for a selection of catalogues (remembering to enclose stamps, SAE or payment if requested), and browse through them in the comfort of your armchair. Catalogues differ considerably, with some having just a list of names, some adding brief descriptions and others describing the plants as fully as possible. There may be suggestions of suitable alpines for particular features, or photographs of a selection of plants. Full-colour catalogues, with pictures of many plants, are rarely produced because of their cost. Many small nurseries produce limited numbers of a wide range of alpines, so their stock can turn round quite rapidly, and they may produce updates or supplements during the year.

If you have not dealt by mail order before, it is probably best to send off for a few plants from two or three nurseries, so that you can see the quality of the plants, how quickly your order is dealt with, and how satisfied you are with their service. You may well find one or two nurseries that you prefer, and after you have ordered you are usually added to their mailing list and will receive new catalogues as they are produced.

Once you start collecting more unusual alpines, you may find that you can only obtain many of them by mail order, or by travelling long distances to particular nurseries. There are many, many alpines only produced by dedicated and specialist growers, often in small quantities.

This collection of alpines, acquired by mail order or by visiting nurseries, is awaiting planting

The sales tables are a wonderful source of new plants for you, and the owners or AGS helpers will willingly answer queries. You can often come across alpines that you may not find elsewhere, especially rarer types, difficult-to-propagate ones, or seed-grown alpines from wild-collected sources.

Specialist societies

National and local groups

We have mentioned the Alpine Garden Society (AGS), a well-established society catering for both the alpine enthusiast and the beginner. The national society also holds lecture days and conferences, at which experienced alpine gardeners talk about specific plants or genera, or various parts of the world they have visited to see alpines growing in the wild. This is an opportunity to meet up with a wider range of like-minded alpine enthusiasts.

The society has numerous local groups that meet once a month or so, to listen to a lecture and view slides, or to visit gardens or nurseries. Local groups are ideal for meeting other alpine gardeners, exchanging news or hearing about plants hitherto unknown to you, asking for advice, or swapping cuttings, seeds or plants.

Specialist groups such as the Cyclamen Society produce their own newsletters, while other societies include the Scottish Rock Garden Club, the New Zealand Alpine Garden Society and the American Rock Garden Society. These can be a wonderful source of information on new and unusual alpines, and an excellent way to obtain seed of alpines you may not find anywhere else.

Alpine shows

In the UK, a number of alpine shows organized by the Alpine Garden Society (AGS) are held in various venues around the country. Amateur growers and exhibitors put on competitive displays of alpines in pots, with classes for beginners and classes for more experienced exhibitors. Shows are held throughout much of the year, and some exhibitors travel many miles to display their prize plants. Specialist nurseries are invited to have selling tables, and the AGS also has its own table selling plants donated by members, who receive a percentage of the price. These shows are an excellent way of viewing a whole range of alpines grown by both keen beginners and very experienced growers. Do bear in mind, though, that some of the desirable cushion specimens and others have been grown in alpine houses and are not suited to growing outside in the garden.

Newsletters and journals

The AGS produces a glossy quarterly bulletin packed with articles, information, stunning photographs of habitats and plants, reports of shows and so on, as well as advertising many specialist nurseries and seed suppliers.

The informative articles are written by a wide range of people, from those who have years of experience and wish to share their knowledge and love of alpines, to keen amateurs who are writing about their first successes. Those who travel to view alpines in the wild describe the habitats and the often difficult treks to reach the plants they have come to see, and individual plants or genera are described, often with helpful cultivation notes. The AGS also has a panel of experts that you can write to for specific advice, and they will do their best to answer your queries.

Part of the competitive display of alpines at an Alpine Garden Society Show in the UK

CULTIVATION

Alpines have long had a reputation as being difficult to grow, requiring the creation of large and expensive rock gardens in which to thrive. This reputation is undeserved: many alpines and rock plants are relatively easy to manage provided that the few basic principles we set out below are followed. Some of the more unusual varieties do have special requirements, but the small size of the plants means that these conditions can often be created even in a small garden, using some of the ideas in the following chapters. If you are unsure of what these plants require, the best guide is to try to recreate as closely as possible the natural conditions in which the plant or its near relatives grow. This is where it helps to know the plant's origins, or at least its natural type of habitat.

Position

The majority of alpines prefer an open sunny position, where the air can move freely around them. Specific groups, such as many of the saxifrages, prefer dappled shade and, in some cases, full shade or a north-facing spot. When siting alpine features you should keep them away from overhanging trees and shrubs, because in the autumn fallen leaves can swamp the small alpines beneath, and heavy water dripping from the leaves and branches will increase the risk of rotting. Shade therefore needs to be provided from a distance.

Oxalis adenophylla **needs a position in full sun**

Left **These saxifrages are thriving in dappled shade**

Soils

Drainage is the most important factor to consider when planting alpines. Few of them will tolerate a lot of moisture around the base of the plant, or constant dampness around the roots. Excess moisture is likely to cause the plant to rot, particularly in the wetter winter months. Ideally, the soil should be free-draining to allow heavy rainfall to dissipate quickly: a top dressing of sharp grit will keep the foliage above the moisture.

Sandy soils, which are usually naturally free-draining, need very little preparation and alpines can often be planted on the level. Very poor sandy soils will sometimes benefit from the addition of small quantities of organic matter, which helps to retain moisture to sustain the plants through hot dry spells.

Heavy soils can be improved by the addition of grit and sharp sand, and in clay soils the addition of organic matter will help to break down the clay and improve drainage. It is difficult on heavy soils, except on a very large scale, to improve the soil enough to plant on the level: if just a small area is improved it tends to act as a sump for the water from the surrounding garden, which only makes the situation worse. The best way is to install a drainage system under the area you wish to improve, although this can be an expensive operation. On this type of soil the best answer is to raise the planting level using a raised bed or similar feature which will allow the water to drain through the soil and out of the base.

If you need to add organic matter to your soil, choose material that is low in nutrients, such as well-made garden compost or some of the proprietary bagged materials. Farmyard manure should be avoided as it is too rich and will encourage undesirable lush growth.

Any grit used for soil improvement needs to be fine, ideally no more than 5mm (¼in) in size. Clean, sharp sand is also very effective, but avoid builder's soft sand as this tends to be so fine that it holds moisture itself.

Top dressings are important for most alpine features. In addition to keeping moisture from the base of the plant, they prevent soil splashing over the foliage during heavy rain and provide an attractive background to the plants. The size of the material needs to be in proportion to the size of the plant, but for most alpines 5mm (¼in) across is ideal. We use flint grit for most of our plantings, but many other materials are suitable such as granite chips, slate waste, or one of the coloured aggregates sold in garden centres. For plants that like lime, such as silver saxifrages and *Dianthus*, fine limestone chippings look effective and also provide a slow release source of lime for the plants. For plantings of acid- or moisture-loving alpines, a fine grade of bark chips can be very effective.

Planting

The ideal times to plant your alpine feature are in the spring or the early autumn. If you have to plant during the summer the plants will need to be watered more frequently in hot weather as their root

Soak the pot in water before planting if the compost is on the dry side

systems will not have spread as far. During a very
hot period they will benefit from shading from the
full heat of the sun until they are more established.
The importance of good initial establishment
cannot be emphasized strongly enough.

Alpines are ideally planted as young well-grown
plants from 7cm or 9cm (3 or 3½in) pots,
allowing their root system to grow away quickly
and spread out through the bed. The roots of
older plants will often remain in the shape of the
pot even when planted out, thus preventing them
from seeking out moisture during dry periods and
causing the premature death of the plant.

Plant alpines by first digging a hole slightly
larger than the pot but no deeper. Make sure the
rootball is moist. If it is on the dry side, soak in a
bucket of water until the compost is well
moistened. Loosen the soil at the base of the hole
and add a small amount of bonemeal. Place the
plant in the hole and fill in the soil around the
rootball, making sure that the crown of the plant
remains on the surface. The rootball should not be
left in a hollow, as this will encourage water to
drain towards the crown. Lightly firm the soil and
then water well to wash it into any air pockets that
may have formed. After watering, the foliage
should be gently lifted and a top dressing about
1cm (½in) deep placed under it so the foliage does
not rest on the soil. On a new feature, top dress
around each plant and then cover the soil between
the plants with top dressing.

If you are planting into an established bed it is
a good idea to scrape the top dressing back before
you begin planting, as this will prevent it becoming
mixed with the soil from your hole. The soil from
the hole should be placed in a bucket rather than
on the surface of the bed to prevent it becoming
mixed with the top dressing.

Right **Lightly firm the soil without compacting it too much**

Dig a hole and remove the plant from its pot

Place the plant in the hole

**Fill in around the rootball with soil, making sure the
crown of the plant is level with the surface**

Watering and feeding

You will find that established alpines, either in the ground or in raised beds over soil, need very little watering. This regime will also encourage the roots to spread down and out in order to find their own water. Only in long, dry spells should you need to water. The soil in a raised bed may drain freely, but the soil underneath, away from the drying effects of the sun, will remain moist in all but the sandiest of conditions and provide a reservoir for the plants above.

Plants growing in containers such as troughs or pots, or in raised beds over a solid base, will need to be watered in dry weather. The amount they require will depend on the plants themselves. Succulent alpines such as sedums and sempervivums will withstand much drier conditions than leafy types such as *Campanula*. We usually water our sinks thoroughly once a fortnight in the summer months and once a week in very hot dry spells. Smaller containers will need more frequent watering.

Alpines will benefit from the addition of small amounts of fertilizer. Avoid over feeding, particularly with nitrogen-rich fertilizers, as it can cause the growth to become very soft and lush, making it much more susceptible to damage. The plants will also look out of character, and spreading plants may easily swamp their smaller neighbours.

We have found that a light annual dressing with a slow-release organic fertilizer such as pelleted poultry manure is very effective. In very wet seasons, when nutrients are leached more rapidly from the soil, then an additional dressing in the early autumn will freshen up the plants before the onset of winter. Care should be taken when applying solid fertilizers as the pellets or granules will quickly scorch the leaves if they are allowed to rest on them. A thorough watering after applying the granules will usually prevent the problem by washing the fertilizer on to the surrounding compost or soil.

Pruning and trimming

Trimming and cutting back is an essential task with many alpines. If they are left to grow unchecked, many will spread and cover fairly large areas, and after a time they will become bare in the centre as the new growth is produced at the tips. Dead-heading is also important as some alpines will multiply prolifically if they are allowed to shed seed. Many alpines will produce further flowers, or a second later flush of flowers, if dead-headed or cut back after flowering.

Many alpines can be trimmed using a sharp pair of secateurs, but for the smaller varieties we have found that good quality pointed scissors are easier to use on fine stems and are less likely to damage tiny leaves or delicate foliage.

Spreading alpines, such as *Gypsophila*, *Phlox* and *Veronica*, should be cut back hard to new shoots at the base once they have finished flowering: this will encourage them to make fresh new growth on which they will flower either later in the season or the following year. Late-flowering varieties such as *Persicaria* and *Frankenia* can be given a light trim to tidy them after flowering, but are best left and given a hard trim in the spring when they begin to shoot.

Shrubby plants such as *Helianthemum*, *Hyssopus* and upright forms of *Thymus* need to be trimmed back hard to new growth when they begin to shoot

Using secateurs to cut back spent flowering stems and woody growth on *Sedum kamtschaticum* **var.** *ellacombeanum*

The tidied plant, showing plenty of fresh new shoots emerging at the base

in the spring. After flowering, a light trim tidies them for the rest of the season, and this often encourages a second flush of flowers, particularly with *Helianthemum*.

Smaller, mound-forming alpines such as *Saxifraga, Draba* and *Armeria* do not usually need trimming. Occasionally an individual rosette will die, and can often be removed by gentle pulling, but sometimes they need to be cut out using a small pair of secateurs or pointed scissors. All of these types of alpine will benefit from having the flowering stems trimmed off completely once the flowers are over in order to keep the plant looking tidy.

Plants that form mats of rosettes such as *Sempervivum* and many *Saxifraga* can be reduced in size simply by trimming off the outer rosettes, although if planted in the right position they seldom outgrow their allotted space. Once they have finished flowering the stems can be cut off. Old flowering stems of *Sempervivum* are best left until they have dried completely, thus preventing disease from entering the plant through the fleshy

wounds. Once dry, they are easy to simply pull away. In sempervivums the individual rosettes that flower eventually turn brown and die. These rosettes can then be carefully pulled from the plant, either with nimble fingers or with a pair of tweezers.

The rosettes on these alpines grow from the centre, gradually leaving a ring of dead, brown leaves around their base. On established plants with small tight rosettes these are usually hidden by the surrounding rosettes, but they can look unsightly on younger plants or those with larger rosettes. On these plants they can be removed by carefully pulling them with fingers or tweezers. This is best done in dry weather, when the papery dried leaves will come away cleanly.

Alpine bulbs should be treated in the same way as other bulbs, dead-heading them once the flowers have finished (unless you want to collect and save seed), and then allowing the foliage to die down naturally before gently pulling it out of the ground.

Remove fallen leaves from small alpines before they cause rotting

Botrytis (grey mould) can spread rapidly, killing shoots, leaves and flowers – remove affected material as soon as possible and destroy it

All alpine features benefit from a regular tidy up. Fallen leaves from surrounding trees and shrubs should be removed regularly, as they can easily swamp a small alpine or cause it to rot. Bird droppings should also be removed before they scorch the foliage. Any damaged shoots on the alpines themselves should be cut off cleanly as soon as possible, to prevent diseases such as *Botrytis* (grey mould) which can rapidly spread through small plants.

Problems, pests and diseases

Drought

Drought can be a problem, particularly in containers in the hot summer months. The first signs are often a dulling of the foliage, which then becomes limp: in very dry conditions this will occur even in succulent alpines such as *Sempervivum* and *Sedum*. If left unwatered, the plants may eventually turn brown and die. Before they have

turned brown, most plants will recover if they are watered and then subsequently kept moist. Sinks and troughs that have become very dry can take some time to re-wet, as any water will tend to run straight through the compost and out of the base. The best solution is to water the soil several times a day until it has taken up enough moisture, and then endeavour to prevent it drying out again.

Waterlogging

In a well-constructed alpine feature waterlogging should not be a problem except in extreme weather conditions. The first symptom is usually the browning of the foliage or the rotting of a rosette. In the short term, the quickest solution for a small bed or a sink or trough is to suspend a clear waterproof cover over the feature to reduce the amount of water falling on the surface and allow the soil to drain. With smaller movable containers, placing them in a cold greenhouse or even a shed or garage will help to dry out the compost. If the problem persists, then the only solution is to rebuild the bed, adding more drainage material, or to replant the trough, adding more grit to the compost. Plants that are suffering badly should be lifted from the bed and potted into some free-draining compost, then kept in a well-ventilated greenhouse or cold frame until they have recovered and the problem with the bed has been overcome.

Sun scorch

Plants such as *Saxifraga* can scorch very quickly in the bright summer sun. The symptoms are usually browning and crisping of the foliage, or shrivelling of rosettes or foliage. The only solution is to provide the plant with some shade, perhaps from a

taller plant or by moving the plant into a shadier area. Make sure you find out about a new plant's requirements before planting to lessen the chance of this problem occurring.

Aphids

A bad attack of aphids, or greenfly, can cause major damage to any alpine, but the damage tends to be greatest on younger plants that are producing soft new growth.

There are numerous types of aphids, with colours ranging from green through red to black, all of which will cause very similar damage.

The first symptom of an attack may be a sticky coating on the young growth. This sticky secretion often becomes coated with a black sooty mould, turning the leaf surface black and unsightly. If an attack is left unchecked, the new leaves can become distorted, resulting in reduced growth, and because of the relatively small size of the plants even a modest attack can cause the death of the plants. It is therefore very important to take remedial action at the first sign of an attack.

There are many insecticides on the market which are effective against aphids. The best ones to use are those which are selective, and not toxic to beneficial insects such as ladybirds and bees. Biological control methods can be equally effective if the problem is caught early. A regular spray with soft soap will reduce the problem quickly and help to lessen the stickiness on the leaves.

Waterlogged soil can cause rotting of roots or top growth – these rosettes have separated from their main roots, although fresh ones are being produced

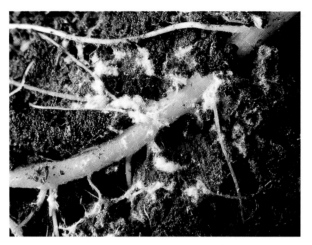

The white fluffy specks characteristic of root aphids

The distinctive white, brown-headed vine weevil larva

Root aphids

Root aphids can sometimes be found in alpines grown in pots, but are only visible when the plants are removed from the pot. They appear around the edges as white specks of a powdery substance: examination will reveal that each contains a small aphid. They rarely have a significant effect on the growth of established plants, usually severely affecting only young seedlings.

Control is difficult, although limited success may be achieved by watering the compost with a spray-strength solution of a spray recommended for leaf and shoot aphids.

Vine weevils

Vine weevil infestation can be devastating in alpine beds. If you find your plants wilting and looking stunted in early to mid-spring, and if drought is obviously not a cause, then vine weevil larvae are the likely culprits. These white, legless grubs, about 1cm (⅜in) long, have distinctive brown heads. If the plants are carefully lifted, the larvae can be found just below the surface of the soil where they chew the roots. If left unchecked, they will eventually separate the plant from its

root system, which is why wilting occurs. It can be difficult to control the larvae with insecticides. Short-term control is possible with special insecticide-treated compost, but this is effective only for the first six months. Biological control is the most effective treatment, treating the compost with nematodes in midsummer. To be effective, the nematodes must be watered on to warm, moist compost (above 12°C or 54°F), where they will seek out the vine weevil larvae, infect and kill them.

If the damage to plants is not too severe when it is first noticed, you can often save the plants. Carefully remove the original soil, destroying any larvae you find, and pot up the plants in fresh, clean compost. Feed and water the plants well to help them re-establish. Once they are growing well they can be replanted in the bed, provided that the soil has either been treated to kill the larvae or has been replaced with a clean mix.

Adult vine weevils can also cause damage, although this tends to be cosmetic, taking the form of small semi circular bites removed from the edges of leaves. While this does little damage to the plant itself, apart from aesthetic considerations, it does serve as a warning to treat the compost to prevent damage by the larvae.

As well as destroying foliage, slugs will attack buds, the damage becoming apparent once the flowers open

Slugs and snails

Slugs and snails have a voracious appetite for soft leafy alpines. The damage they cause can range from holes in the edges and centre of leaves to the complete destruction of all top-growth on leafy plants such as *Aubrieta, Campanula* and *Erodium*. The tight mats or hummocks of many alpines, such as *Sempervivum* and *Saxifraga*, provide a shelter for slugs in particular, and they often repay their hosts by eating away the fleshy stems and separating the hummocks or mats from their roots.

Slugs and snails can be readily controlled with the various brands of slug pellets, but non-chemical methods can be just as effective. The use of sharp grit as a top dressing is unpleasant to the soft bodies of slugs, making a good deterrent. The grit should be placed under the hummock or mat of foliage to discourage slugs from seeking shelter beneath. In large alpine beds, it is possible to install slug traps baited with liquid such as beer. Treating the bed with nematodes that infect and kill the slugs is another effective method. The nematodes can be applied in the spring once the soil temperature rises

above 5°C (40° F). They will remain active for up to six weeks if the compost is kept moist.

Ants

Ants will cause damage to small alpines when they build their nests nearby. This results in a mound of very fine soil that builds up, quickly swamping the foliage of the plant and, if left unchecked, burying a small plant completely. Ants' nests should be carefully removed as soon as they are seen and the ants treated with a proprietary ant killer.

Mice

In our experience mice can rapidly develop a taste for small bulbs and tubers, and if not controlled they will search out and eat bulbs in a bed. They are also attracted to the tubers of deciduous *Lewisia*, grown in beds or pots. Raised beds and containers are the most susceptible, probably because the well-drained soil is easy to dig. There is a vast array of mousetraps available, which are mostly very effective – although none as effective as our two cats.

Lewisia cotyledon

CHAPTER FOUR

PROPAGATION

Propagating your own alpines from seeds or cuttings is one of the most satisfying aspects of gardening. It is also an excellent way to increase your collection of plants, allowing you to provide specimens to swap with friends and to grow many unusual varieties from local or overseas seed sources.

Seeds

Buying seeds

Seeds can be bought from a wide variety of sources. Many of the large general seed companies include a few of the more popular alpines in their catalogues, but the widest range can usually be obtained from smaller firms, which will include more interesting and challenging species in their lists. Many alpine plant nurseries also produce lists of their own collected seed, and many of these are gems that will not be listed anywhere else. Many of the choice alpines produce only small amounts of seed each year, and the seed is therefore often in short supply. It certainly pays to get your order in early to be sure of getting the best varieties. Many of these small companies now have websites, and we have found several interesting new sources in this way.

If you are interested in more unusual or rare varieties, a good way to obtain seeds is to buy shares in a seed-collecting expedition. These expeditions are organized by individuals or groups to particular regions, such as the Himalayas or Andes, and to pay for the costs of the trip they sell shares in the seeds they collect to individuals. Most expeditions produce a prospectus outlining the trip and providing an indication of the plants from which they hope to collect seed. In return for your share, you will receive a stated division of packets of seed, although the species and numbers will vary considerably and can never be guaranteed. We have participated in several shares in expeditions and have gained some exciting plants as a result.

Many specialist societies run seed exchange schemes whereby members can obtain seed donated by other members. In most schemes you will be able to claim more seed if you are also a seed donor. This can be an excellent way to obtain new varieties, although care is needed with nomenclature: the varying knowledge of the donors may lead to misnaming.

Collecting your own seeds

Collecting and sowing your own seed is a good way to increase many alpines. Collecting more seed than you need is a good idea, as it then allows you

Carefully cut off ripened seed-heads

Place the seed-heads in a container

to swap with other enthusiasts and to become a seed donor in a seed exchange as mentioned above.

If you are collecting seed from the open garden it is important to realize that not all plants will come true from seed. Many plant species (for example, *Aquilegia*) will readily hybridise unless they are kept well away from relatives. This hybridization and variation can, however, result in exciting new varieties.

Seed is best collected as soon as it is ripe, or, in the case of wind-dispersed seed such as *Anemone*, just before this stage. The best way to judge ripeness is to brush the plant gently with your hand: if the seed comes away, it is ready to collect. It may not feel completely dry, but – particularly with wind-dispersed seed – if you leave it any longer it will blow away!

It is best to cut the seed-heads carefully from the plant and place them in a flat tray, as with small alpine seed-heads it is usually not practical to try to remove them in situ. The seeds should be

carefully labelled and then placed in a warm, dry atmosphere to dry gently. Once the seed-heads and stems have become completely dry, they need to be cleaned in order to separate the seeds from the chaff before storage.

Cleaning seeds

Seed can be cleaned in several different ways. Larger seeds such as *Lewisia* or *Sisyrinchium* can usually be separated by gently rubbing the seed-heads between the fingers and allowing the seeds to fall into a clean tray. We have found that small photographic developing trays are ideal, as they incorporate a small spout which allows the cleaned seeds to be poured into packets.

Separate smaller seeds by shaking through a series of sieves until the seed and chaff have been separated. Kitchen sieves are ideal for this: we now have a collection of six or seven different ones, each with different-sized mesh, together with one

Separate seeds from chaff by sieving – use a variety of mesh sizes to clean the seed as much as possible

or two home-made sieves consisting of a simple wooden frame and metal mesh such as zinc gauze.

Carefully blowing over the surface of the tray of seed and chaff can be a very effective way of separating seeds from light chaff, but care is needed as too much force can blow the seeds themselves away.

Wind-dispersed seeds such as *Anemone* and *Pulsatilla* are usually very small, but are attached to light, larger structures to carry them in the wind. If you are patient you can carefully separate the two, but it is a very tedious process. In our experience it is rarely worthwhile, and provided that the seeds are well distributed when they are sown, germination is not usually affected.

Once the seeds have been cleaned, they should be sown as soon as possible, so that they do not dry out completely. If you are going to store them, they should be placed in small packets and stored in a cool, dry place. The best packets for this are small waxed envelopes of the type sold to stamp collectors, as these have a

good seal at the base but are not completely airtight when closed at the top. (Postal envelopes are not ideal as they are rarely sealed completely at the base, and this can allow leakage.) Always label packets clearly with the name of the plant and the date collected.

Conditions for germination

Alpines are very variable in their germination times, ranging from a few weeks to a year or more. The greatest success usually results from mimicking nature as much as possible. Storing seeds for a long period of time can result in their drying out and taking a lot longer to germinate. In our experience, sowing most seeds in early winter produces good results, allowing the seed pans to experience the fluctuations in temperature that they would receive naturally. Germination will then begin in early spring and continue through the year, depending on the species.

Sowing seeds

Some alpine seeds can take a considerable time to germinate, and because of this it is important that they are sown onto compost that drains freely while retaining enough moisture to allow the seedlings to develop once they germinate.

The mixture that we recommend for the majority of alpines is a mix of John Innes No. I, a good quality peat-based seed compost and fine flint grit in equal proportions. For smaller, choicer species, equal proportions of John Innes No. I and fine flint grit is ideal.

Use ordinary pots or deep pans for sowing most seeds, as the extra depth compared to a seed tray helps to prevent the compost drying out completely in hot weather.

1 Fill the pot with compost to within about 1cm (½in) of the top.
2 Gently firm the compost to produce a level surface.
3 Spread the seed evenly over the surface.
   If the seed is very small, cover the compost with a thin layer of silver sand before sowing – the fine seed will then be visible as it is spread.
4 Cover the seed with a layer of about 1cm (½in) of flint grit. Compost should not be used, as it will tend to produce a cap through which the tiny seedlings have trouble emerging.
5 Label the pot with the variety and date sown, and the source of seed if appropriate.
6 Water the pots carefully, using a watering can with an upturned rose to give a finer spray.

Once the seeds have been sown, the pots should be placed in a cold frame or in an unheated greenhouse. They should be watered sparingly and never allowed to dry out completely or become waterlogged.

Pots of seed are best covered in a layer of flint grit

Pots of seed in a cold frame (the *Cyclamen* are in their second year and ready for potting)

Mousetraps are a good idea to save your seed from being dug up!

Care of seedlings

Once the seedlings begin to emerge they should be monitored carefully, and as soon as they are large enough to handle they should be pricked on into individual pots. Care needs to be taken when handling the tiny seedlings. Hold them by their leaves, not the stem: damaged leaves will be replaced, but once the stem is damaged the seedling will die. Prick the seedlings into a compost mix of half John Innes No. 2 and half peat-based compost, dibbing them in carefully, and then top dress the compost with flint grit. The young seedlings are very vulnerable to scorch and should be placed in a shaded environment until they have become established and hardened off. They are also very prone to damage from slugs and snails, which should be controlled either with pellets or the use of traps.

A pot of *Gentiana acaulis* **seedlings, ready for pricking out**

Alpine cuttings need nimble fingers and sharp tools – *Sedum spathulifolium* **roots readily from individual rosettes taken as cuttings**

Propagation by cuttings

Cuttings are an easy way to propagate many alpines. One of the advantages of taking cuttings is that the new plants will all be the same as the parent. Alpine cuttings are very small, and so they need nimble fingers, small tools and more care than with larger plants.

Composts for cuttings

The basic medium for a good cutting compost is a fine-to-medium sphagnum peat, to which can be added a range of materials such as perlite, flint grit, silver sand or very fine bark. The mix that we prefer for most alpines is one part of peat to one part of fine flint grit. This provides excellent results with a wide range of subjects. The mixture is very well drained and gives good support for the small cuttings.

Types of cutting

One of the most important factors in the successful rooting of cuttings is the time in the plants' growth cycle that the cuttings are taken. Alpines root successfully from stem or shoot cuttings taken when the growth is soft and new (softwood), or taken just as the shoots begin to firm (semi-hardwood).

Softwood cuttings are usually taken in the spring as the plant begins to grow, but if necessary they can be taken at any time provided that the growth is soft and new. Semi-hardwood or semi-ripe cuttings are normally used in summer or early autumn. The older material takes longer to root, but it is more robust and less prone to rotting and disease in the cooler autumn and winter months.

Root cuttings are a good way to multiply several alpine species, notably *Primula* and *Pulsatilla*. These are usually taken from young fleshy roots in late winter.

Facilities for cuttings

Cuttings need to be enclosed to maintain humidity and prevent wilting. There are many different ways of doing this, ranging from simple home-made frames covered in polythene to the specially designed, thermostatically controlled units available from garden centres. A well-made cold frame can also be used, particularly for semi-hardwood and root cuttings.

The small size of alpines means that normal secateurs are too large for preparing cuttings. We have found that a pair of sharp-pointed scissors is ideal: if kept sharp they will make a clean cut on even the finest stem. They should be thoroughly cleaned after use to prevent the spread of disease.

For small numbers of cuttings, square pots are ideal containers. A 7cm (3in) pot will hold six to nine cuttings, depending upon the plant, while for larger numbers, small seed trays are ideal. In our experience it is not a good idea to put different cuttings in the same tray, as they rarely root at the same rate, resulting in problems when one of them is ready to pot on and not the other. Whatever containers are used, they should either be new or thoroughly cleaned and sterilized before use.

Taking the cuttings

Softwood cuttings

1 Fill a pot or tray with compost to within 1cm (½in) of the top. The compost should be firmed gently to provide a level surface. (A small piece of board cut to fit the pot or tray is ideal for this.)

2 The cutting material should be collected from the plant and placed in a polythene bag. When collecting, cut them longer than required so that they can be finally prepared immediately before insertion. Softwood cuttings will wilt rapidly once collected, so they should be inserted as quickly as possible.

3 The finished cuttings should ideally have two to three pairs of leaves below the tip. Prepare the cuttings by carefully removing the lower leaves with sharp scissors or secateurs, and then trim the stem to leave about 0.5–1cm (¼–½in) to insert in the compost, making sure that you include at least one leaf node. For plants with rosettes, such as *Saxifraga*, it is usually sufficient to remove old leaves from the base of the rosette and then insert the remaining stem in the compost.

Carefully remove lower leaves from the cutting

A batch of prepared cuttings of *Veronica pectinata*

Press the cuttings into the compost and gently firm around them

The completed, labelled pot of cuttings

4 Dip the stem into a rooting compound. have found that a liquid hormone is the most effective, as you cannot use too much. Use a hormone that has an added fungicide if possible, as this will help to prevent rotting at the base of the shoot.

5 Press the cuttings into the compost, but do not firm them in: only with very weak stems should it be necessary to use a dibber to make a hole and carefully fill it around the cutting. Space the cuttings out well so that they do not touch each other and have room to grow once they have rooted.

6 When the pot or tray is full, water it thoroughly using a light spray so as not to disturb the cuttings. The watering will also firm the compost around the cuttings.

7 Place the cuttings in a closed propagator as soon as possible to prevent them wilting. Early in the spring they will benefit from gentle bottom heat, but as the weather warms up this is unnecessary.

8 The atmosphere must be kept humid to prevent the cuttings from wilting. If you only have a small number of cuttings in a large propagator it is a good idea to add a tray of sand or compost, which can also be kept wet to help maintain the humidity.

9 Protect the cuttings from the sun by shading the propagator. Removable shade netting is ideal, as it can be taken off during dull weather.

Semi-hardwood cuttings

For semi-hardwood cuttings, follow the steps as for softwood cuttings until the end of step 6. Semi-hardwood cuttings do not need as much humidity as softwood cuttings, and in late summer and autumn will usually root well if placed on a shaded bench in a cold greenhouse or in a shaded cold frame. If the cuttings show signs of wilting, a sheet of thin polythene supported over them for the first week or two will generally firm them up.

Root cuttings

Root cuttings are most successful if taken in late winter, just before the roots begin active growth.

1 Carefully lift the plant you wish to propagate and tease the soil away from the roots. Choosing the youngest, fattest roots cut them cleanly near to the base of the plant. Leave about half the roots untouched to allow the plant to re-establish.

2 Wash the root sections carefully to remove most of the soil. Each root can then be cut into sections about 2cm (1in) long. It is important to be able to identify the top of the root – a good way of doing this is to make a horizontal cut at the top of the section and a sloping cut at the base. On some roots such as *Geranium*, tiny buds or lumps will be visible, and at least one of these should be included in each section if possible.

3 The cuttings can then be inserted vertically in pots of cutting compost, so that the top of the cutting is just below the surface of the compost. Water the pots well to settle the compost.

4 The cuttings will root and subsequently shoot over several months if left in a cool place. This can be reduced to four to five weeks in many cases if gentle bottom heat is used (70–75°F; 21–24°C).

The care and growing on of cuttings

The aftercare of cuttings is as important as how they are taken. The cuttings must be kept moist throughout the rooting process. If they are watered well they are unlikely to need any more water until they have begun to root, but do keep a careful check (particularly with cuttings on the greenhouse bench or in a cold frame), and give a little water when required. The cuttings should also be checked frequently for any signs of disease and any affected leaves removed immediately. Grey mould (*Botrytis*) will spread rapidly through a pot of cuttings if infected material is not removed immediately. The first sign of rooting is usually a freshening of the foliage, with new growth beginning, and a resistance when the cutting is gently pulled usually confirms that rooting has started.

Once rooted, the cuttings need to be weaned slowly from their enclosed environment. The best way to do this is gradually to increase the ventilation over several days, allowing the new young plants to acclimatize.

Once the cuttings have been weaned they will benefit from a feed with a dilute solution of a tomato fertilizer. When the cuttings are growing well they can be potted up into individual pots. Timing is important and the aim should be to pot the cuttings when they are making active root growth, or the roots will just sit in new compost and can rot very quickly. In practice this means avoiding the winter period. Good quality alpine compost should be used. We have found that a mix of equal parts of John Innes No. 2 and a good quality peat-based compost is a good base to which can be added varying amounts of flint grit according to the plants' needs.

Newly potted cuttings need to be watered carefully, as the soft new roots are very vulnerable either to drying out, or to rotting if they are allowed to become too wet. Once potted, the cuttings should be left to establish, being planted into their final positions once roots are visible at the bottom of the pot and they are growing strongly.

Use a trowel to separate and dig up part of an established clump (this is *Sisyrinchium idahoense*)

Carefully remove excess soil to make division of the clump easier to manage

Division

One of the easiest ways to propagate alpines is by division, and their diminutive size makes this a simple process.

1 Carefully lift the chosen plant and gently remove excess soil from the roots.

2 Many plants can simply be pulled apart, taking care to tease out any tangled roots. A steady shaking and pulling is usually effective.

3 Avoid breaking the plant into very small pieces: although these may each have roots they will be slow to develop and often fail completely. Larger clumps will grow away quickly once potted and can, if necessary, be divided again later in the season. If the divisions are large enough, they can be planted directly into their final positions, provided they are watered well until they become established.

4 Plants with woody stems such as *Thymus serpyllum* should be carefully cut into sections using sharp secateurs, making sure that each portion has some roots attached.

5 The divisions should be potted up and grown on as for cuttings, although they will normally be ready to plant out much sooner than cuttings.

Separate pieces of plant, making sure that each piece has sufficient roots

Pot up individual divided pieces

Suggestions for easy and more challenging alpines to propagate

Seed

Easy	More challenging
Acinos alpinus	Aethionema
Aquilegia flabellata 'Ministar'	Campanula
Dianthus deltoides (and forms)	(seed is very tiny)
Epilobium crassum	Gentiana acaulis
Lewisia cotyledon	Townsendia
Linum perenne 'Blau Saphir'	
Papaver alpinum	
Saponaria ocymoides	
Scutellaria	

Cuttings

Easy	More challenging
Achillea 'Huteri'	Artemisia
Dianthus	Asperula
Hypericum olympicum	Erodium
Saxifraga 'Winifred Bevington'	Penstemon pinifolius
Saxifraga × urbium	Pterocephalus perennis
Sedum spurium	Silene acaulis
Thymus	

Division

Easy
Antennaria
Aruncus aethusifolius
Campanula 'Birch Hybrid'
Leptinella
Sempervivum (by rooted offsets)
Sisyrinchium

CHAPTER FIVE

RAISED BEDS

An excellent way of ensuring better drainage for alpines is to grow them in a bed raised above the surrounding ground level. Raised beds can be constructed from a variety of materials and can be made in different shapes and sizes to suit your particular garden. The soil used for filling the bed can be mixed to provide better drainage around the plant roots than ordinary garden soil, and, together with the free drainage from a higher level, allows a great variety of alpines to be grown.

Advantages of raised beds

By choosing the position of the bed and the type of soil you use conditions can be created to grow a very wide range of plants. Being raised above ground level allows much freer drainage around the roots of plants. They must not be allowed to dry out, but sharp drainage means that the roots and necks are not sitting in water during wet periods. This is especially important for many alpines, as we have already discussed. The plants can also be appreciated

Left **An attractive brick raised bed filled with alpines and miniature conifers, the sides softened by additional planting at the base**

more when raised above ground level, particularly as they are small in scale anyway.

It is much easier to maintain the plants, as they are contained in a limited area and are nearer to hand for working on. This is especially important for the elderly or for those with disabilities, as it requires less stooping.

Sizes and shapes

The advantage of raised beds is that they can be built specifically to the shape and size you require, and can be fitted into all sorts of places in the garden. Use a raised bed to separate the patio from the lawn, as a feature alongside a path, to create interest in a flat site, or as a division between two different levels in the garden.

The size of a raised bed will be determined by the area you have available and the scale of your garden, as well as the number of alpines you wish to grow. You may prefer to have several smaller raised beds rather than a single large one. A group of low raised beds surrounded by gravel, perhaps with a few planted containers of alpines among them, can make a very attractive feature. Make sure that the bed is of a size that you can cope with and that it can be reached easily all round for maintaining.

Small-scale plants such as *Saponaria* × *olivana* **can be appreciated more when raised above ground level**

A minimum height of 25cm (10in) is recommended, and any height up to about 60cm (24in), although soil settlement may become a problem at this depth. Raised beds can be made to a suitable height for the disabled or elderly, so that they can be reached easily from a wheelchair or without having to bend too much. It is especially important in these cases not to make the bed too wide, but just wide enough to be accessible from all round.

A raised bed can be square, rectangular or L-shaped, depending upon the material it is constructed from. If it is built from stone, brick or log rolls it can be gently curved. It can also be built in shallow tiers. Construct your bed to a size easily accessible from all around or from one or more sides, so that you can reach the centre without overstretching. If you want a wider bed, you can put stepping stones across it, but don't forget that this will compact the soil.

Building a raised bed

A well-constructed bed will last many years, so it is worth spending some time and effort on the initial construction. Positioning the bed is important: an open position is ideal, but a shady spot can work well provided that it is planted with shade-loving plants. Overhanging trees and shrubs should be avoided if at all possible to reduce the problem of fallen leaves and too much dense shade. Once the site has been chosen it should be cleared of all perennial weeds, either by using a systemic herbicide such as glyphosate or by digging out the weeds and all their roots. With the site cleared, construction can begin.

Methods of construction

The appearance of your raised bed depends largely on the material you use for the retaining walls. This will be determined by the effect you want to create, the amount you want to spend on it, and whether you want a formal or more rustic or natural-looking bed. The bed should blend or fit in with your garden setting.

Bricks

These make neat raised beds that are very satisfactory in small or urban gardens, although they are also attractive in rural gardens when old, weathered bricks can be used. Occasional gaps can be left in the sides to accommodate alpines, which will soften the effect. The walls of the bed must be built on a concrete strip foundation with a minimum depth of 20cm (8in) to prevent them from cracking.

Reconstituted stone 'bricks'

These are lighter and are manufactured in various neutral colours. They are suitable for neat beds in paved or urban gardens, or adjacent to areas of patio or path constructed from similar material. Make sure the colour blends or harmonizes with its setting, and remember that reconstituted stone weathers more slowly than brick or natural stone. As with bricks, the wall must be built on a concrete strip foundation.

Railway sleepers

Second-hand railway sleepers make very good retaining walls for larger raised beds. They are extremely heavy and about 2.5 metres (8ft) long, although they can be cut using a chainsaw. Place lengthways on their side and hold the corners firmly together with metal brackets on the inside. Make sure that sleepers are not oozing tar, which is detrimental to plant growth. You can make deeper beds by stacking the sleepers, but they must be securely held in place with metal brackets.

Second-hand railway sleepers make excellent raised beds

A newly planted bed with a top dressing of flint grit

This established raised bed blends effortlessly into the surrounding garden

free-draining garden soil, then use that rather than bringing any in. For alpines needing perfect drainage, the amount of grit can be increased.

For ericaceous plants the soil mixture should be based on a good quality sphagnum peat, to which can be added either lime-free grit or, if very acid conditions are required, fine composted bark chippings. Sieved leaf mould can be substituted for peat in the case of woodland plantings.

After adding the soil layer, the bed should be watered, and this will begin to settle the soil. Whenever possible the bed should then be left for several weeks to settle completely. Prior to planting, more soil can be added if necessary.

Layer 3. Top dressing

The top dressing layer provides a background to the small plants and also improves the drainage immediately at the base of the plant. For most alpines the ideal material is 3–5mm (⅛–³⁄₁₆in) grit including granite, slate, limestone, flint and various coloured types. All of these are equally effective. For most of our beds we use flint grit, since it blends well in our garden. Whichever grit you choose, apply a layer about 1–2cm (³⁄₈–¾in) deep. With a new bed it is easier to plant up the bed before adding the top dressing, which can then be carefully placed around and under the new plants.

Ericaceous plantings can be top dressed with fine bark chippings.

Maintenance

Apart from the plants' requirements, established beds will need little maintenance. In the first season the bed should be watered well in hot dry weather, but once the plants become established their roots will reach the soil beneath the bed and obtain enough water in all but the most extreme conditions.

The top dressing grit is ideal for seed germination and the seeds of many alpines will germinate freely. These must be controlled, or more vigorous species will quickly swamp the slower ones. The easiest way is to dead-head the plants and prevent them seeding, but failing this the seedlings can usually be pulled out easily (and either potted up to use elsewhere or given away). Weed seedlings should also be regularly removed.

Established beds will benefit from a light feed each season, using a slow-release fertilizer such as dried poultry manure. Care should be taken to keep the pellets or granules away from the plants, as they can easily scorch delicate foliage.

Ideas for plants, planting schemes or associations

✳ **All year round interest**
Use coloured and variegated foliage together with a spread of flowering season, and mix with dwarf shrubs and miniature conifers if you wish, using some evergreens to maintain structure and interest over winter.

✳ **Spring or autumn interest**
Choose alpines for specific seasonal interest. Create spring colour by planting *Pulsatilla*, *Primula*, early flowering saxifrages, *Veronica pectinata*, *Armeria* and *Phlox*, as well as spring-flowering miniature bulbs. Alpines flowering in late summer and autumn include *Persicaria*, *Campanula*, *Sedum*, *Geranium*, *Limonium*, *Parahebe*, *Pterocephalus*, *Erodium*, *Scutellaria*, *Scabiosa* and *Solidago*.

✳ **Particular alpine collections**
You may like to collect plants from a particular region or country, or put together a collection of alpines belonging to one genus, such as *Dianthus*, *Saxifraga* or *Sempervivum*.

A colourful collection for all year interest – *Aster alpinus* **flowering in early summer, with silvery** *Erodium chrysanthum* **and a mound of** *Sedum kamtschaticum* **var.** *ellacombeanum* **coming into bud**

Above The goblet-shaped flowers of *Pulsatilla vulgaris* give a wonderful spring display

Right Many sedums, such as *Sedum spurium* 'Purpurteppich', provide stunning displays in late summer and autumn

Left A collection of early flowering saxifrages in a terracotta pan – they all require the same compost and conditions, so are ideal to grow together

* **Ten suggested plants for beginners to try on a raised bed**

    Anemone caroliniana

    Armeria juniperifolia 'Bevan's Variety'

    Campanula 'Birch Hybrid'

    Dianthus 'Dainty Dame'

    Frankenia thymifolia

    Gentiana septemfida

    Helianthemum (any named hybrid)

    Parahebe lyallii 'Julie-Anne'

    Penstemon pinifolius

    Veronica prostrata 'Blue Sheen'

Campanula 'Birch Hybrid' is a reliable, long-flowering alpine, ideal for beginners

* **Ten unusual or challenging plants for keen gardeners**

    Aquilegia laramiensis

    Asperula gussonei

    Dianthus callizonus

    Erigeron compositus var. *discoideus*

    Hypericum empetrifolium subsp. *tortuosum*

    Linum 'Gemmell's Hybrid'

    Minuartia circassica

    Origanum microphyllum

    Phyteuma scheuchzeri

    Potentilla nitida

Dianthus callizonus is a choice species requiring sharp, gritty soil to grow well

Dodecatheon meadia is a stunning plant to grow in a peat bed

* **Ten alpines to use in a peat bed**

    Plant together with dwarf ericaceous shrubs such as *Rhododendron, Cassiope, Kalmiopsis* and *Vaccinium*, for instance.

    Calceolaria tenella

    Dodecatheon meadia

    Gentiana ternifolia 'Dali'

    Gentiana sino-ornata 'Mary Lyle'

    Geum pentapetalum

    Mitella caulescens

    Primula frondosa

    Saxifrage × urbium 'Clarence Elliott'

    Soldanella villosa

    Thalictrum kiusianum

Raised bed *Illustrated in summer*

Plants

1. *Dianthus* 'Dainty Dame'
2. *Convolvulus lineatus*
3. *Dianthus* 'Whatfield Joy'
4. *Scabiosa japonica* var. *alpina*
5. *Penstemon pinifolius* 'Wisley Flame'
6. *Sedum spurium* 'Purpurteppich'
7. *Persicaria vaccinifolia*
8. *Pterocephalus perennis*
9. *Erigeron compositus* var. *discoideus*
10. *Oxalis adenophylla*
11. *Veronica pinnata* 'Blue Eyes'
12. *Berberis* × *stenophylla* 'Corallina Compacta'
13. *Limonium bellidifolium*
14. *Anacyclus pyrethrum* var. *depressus*
15. *Erinus alpinus*
16. *Silene alpestris* 'Flore Pleno'
17. *Potentilla eriocarpa*
18. *Minuartia circassica*
19. *Sempervivum* 'King George'
20. *Phyteuma scheuchzeri*
21. *Veronica prostrata* 'Blue Sheen'
22. *Solidago multiradiata*
23. *Sedum oreganum*
24. *Campanula* 'Birch Hybrid'
25. *Phlox subulata* 'Amazing Grace'

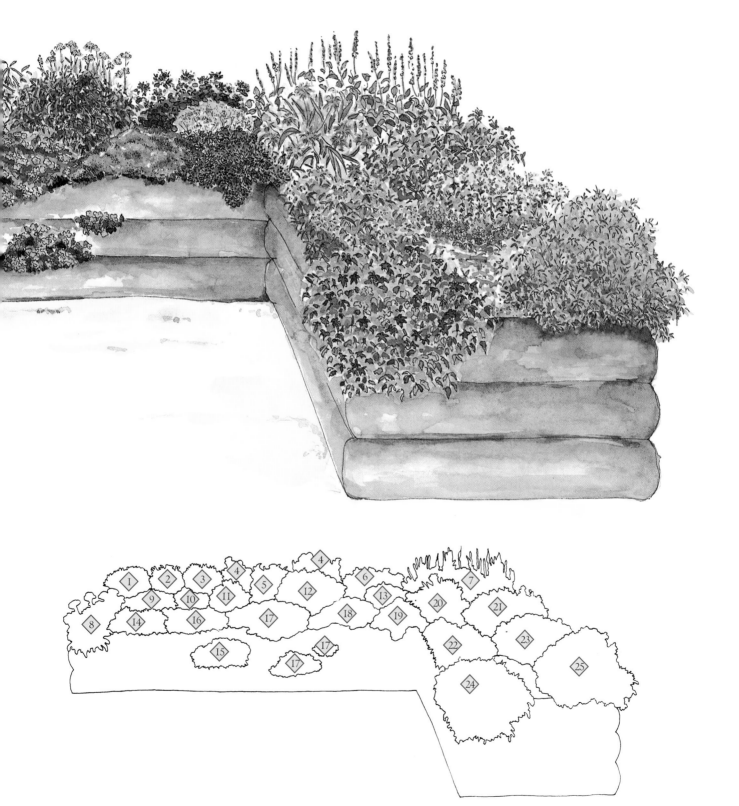

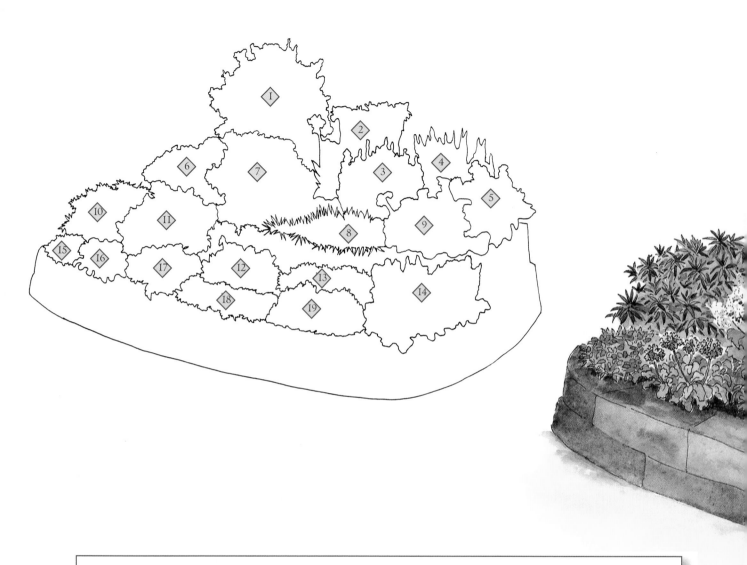

Plants

◇1 *Betula nana*

◇2 *Dodecatheon pulchellum*

◇3 *Cassiope* 'Edinburgh'

◇4 × *Phylliopsis hillieri* 'Pinocchio'

◇5 *Primula frondosa*

◇6 *Salix retusa*

◇7 *Aruncus aethusifolius*

◇8 *Gentiana sino-ornata*

◇9 *Soldanella villosa*

◇10 *Rhododendron impeditum*

◇11 *Tiarella wherryi*

◇12 *Dodecatheon dentatum*

◇13 *Calceolaria* 'John Innes'

◇14 *Mitella breweri*

◇15 *Calceolaria tenella*

◇16 *Primula farinosa*

◇17 *Thalictrum kiusianum*

◇18 *Trollius pumilus*

◇19 *Cassiope* 'Badenoch'

Peat bed *Illustrated in mid–late spring*

TROUGHS AND OTHER CONTAINERS

Trough and container gardens are an ideal way of growing a wide range of small, compact alpines. Several can be fitted into a small area, so they are suitable for those with limited space. They can be filled with different soil mixes and can be placed in sun, partial shade or full shade, creating a range of different conditions for particular groups of plants.

Sinks and troughs

Sinks and troughs can be found in a wide range of sizes and shapes. Some of the most attractive ones are carved from solid rock: these are very durable and will last for several lifetimes without maintenance. The easiest and cheapest ones to obtain are usually old glazed porcelain sinks. To get the best price, ask for damaged ones that cannot be reused indoors. These sinks are usually white and look very stark if used as they are. To give them a natural weathered look, they can easily be coated with a cement mixture known as hypertufa, which is simply a mixture of peat, sand and cement in equal parts.

Coating with hypertufa

1   Before coating the sink, carefully remove any plumbing still attached, taking care not to crack the sink.
2   Clean and wash the sink thoroughly, using detergent to remove any grease and loose glaze.
3   Move the sink as near as possible to its intended position (moving after treatment could damage the coating). Make sure that it is stable.
4   To assist the hypertufa in bonding, coat the sink with plasterer's bonding agent (PVA adhesive) mixed according to the instructions:

This white glazed sink looks rather stark in a garden setting

Left **An attractively planted trough**

an average-sized sink will require about 2–3 tablespoons of bonding agent. The addition of a small amount of sand to the mixture provides a rougher surface and makes the coating process easier. Leave the glue to dry.

5   The hypertufa mix is prepared by mixing sand, peat and cement in the ratio 1:1:1 (by volume), adding enough water to give a smooth firm texture. Adding less peat to the mix will make the mixture slightly harder, and this is a good idea if you intend to move the sink after it has been coated. The final colour of the coating depends on the sand used, and we have found that red pit sand gives a pleasant dark colour.

6   Apply the mixture to the sink using a small builder's trowel. It will adhere better if it is gently pressed onto the surface. Work from the top, down the outside and then over the lip and about 5cm (2in) down the inside of the sink to ensure no glaze is visible when the soil is added. The surface should be left rough to give a more natural appearance and to speed up the weathering process.

7   The coated sink needs to be left for at least a week to allow the hypertufa to harden. If rain threatens during the first day, gently cover the sink with polythene, supporting it in the middle to prevent damage to the coating.

Weathering will gradually mellow the surface of the hypertufa giving it a more natural appearance. This process can be speeded up if desired by painting the surface with a solution of yoghurt in water.

This hypertufa-coated sink has weathered to give a more natural appearance

Left **Cover the drainage hole with perforated zinc**

Place a layer of coarse grit in the base

Filling a trough

It is important to position the trough before it is filled, because once it is full it will be too heavy to move. Support the trough on bricks, concrete blocks or stone to raise it above ground level, with a slight slope towards the drainage hole. The height of the supports can be chosen to suit the situation and proportions of the trough. The supports should be placed on a solid base, and if the soil beneath has been recently dug it should be firmed down well to prevent the supports sinking in.

The drainage hole in the trough should be covered with a piece of perforated zinc (available from hardware stores), which helps to keep some

pests out while allowing drainage and preventing the compost from falling through.

The trough should then be filled in layers as follows:

1 A drainage layer of coarse grit, broken crocks or finely crushed bricks to a depth of up to 5cm (2in) in deep troughs. In very shallow troughs of 5–8cm (2–3¼in) this layer is best left out and extra grit added to the compost layer.

2 A compost mixture to within 3cm (1in) of the top of the trough. A good general compost for most alpines is a mixture of John Innes compost, peat-based compost, and grit in equal proportions, plus a small quantity of bonemeal. The mixture can be adjusted according to the requirements of your plants. Add a greater proportion of grit for more scree-like conditions, and use an ericaceous compost for lime-hating plants. The compost should be watered well and then left for several days to settle.

3 A top dressing to within 1cm (½in) of the top of the trough. We have found that 3–5mm (⅛–³⁄₁₆in) flint grit makes an attractive dressing for use with most plants, and for ericaceous plantings fine bark chippings are very effective.

Fill the sink with an alpine compost mixture

Plant selection

When choosing plants for your trough, take care to ensure that they are all compact and slow-growing forms, which will blend together and not swamp each other within a few months. A carefully planned scheme should last for many years with only the minimum of maintenance.

A sketch plan is an invaluable aid to help visualize the arrangement and to select the number of plants. When designing the layout, use plants of varying growth habits to prevent a flat appearance. Keep taller plants towards a corner rather than right in the centre, and use trailing and prostrate plants to hang over the sides. Rocks or tufa can be used to create further interest and add height to the planting. In shallow sinks, the compost can be built up between the pieces of rock to create greater depth for the roots of the plants. Rock can also provide a cooler root-run for the plants – particularly important if the sink is in full sun. Plants around and between the rock or tufa will gradually grow over the edges to soften the effect.

An established trough planting, with *Juniperus communis* 'Compressa' (many years old!), and alpines of varying habit and flowering period

These planted troughs blend in and add interest to the surrounding planting

Many different planting themes can be used. Miniature landscapes, with perhaps a dwarf conifer, some rock or tufa, and plants of complementary shapes and colours, provide interesting features, while colourful arrangements of plants (either for a mass display of flowers at one time, or with flowering periods spaced over the year) would brighten a dull corner. Collections of one particular sort of plant such as sempervivums or saxifrages in several varieties also make attractive features.

Planting

A good time to do the planting is in the spring or early autumn, but not in adverse weather conditions when the compost is frozen or waterlogged. If you have already bought your plants, they can be kept in a sheltered spot, greenhouse or frame, or even in a shed or porch for a short while, until conditions have improved.

Lay out the plants in their pots on the surface of the compost, rearranging them until you are happy with the result

Stages in planting

1 Lay the plants out on the sink in their pots, together with any rocks you plan to include. Rearrange them until you are happy with the final effect.

2 Position the rocks by burying about one-third beneath the compost – this will anchor them in place, and will allow tufa (if you are using it) to absorb moisture from the compost.

3 Ensure that the new plants are moist before planting. If they are on the dry side, stand them in a bucket or bowl of water until the compost is well moistened.

4 Using a small trowel make a planting hole slightly larger than the rootball, remove the plant from its pot, place it in the hole and gently fill the hole with the surrounding compost. Ensure that the crown of the plant is above the surface of the compost. Firm the compost gently around the plant. Repeat with the remaining plants.

5 When you have completed planting, level the compost to just within 3cm (1in) of the top of the trough. Water the plants in well.

6 Top dress the sink with a 1–2cm (⅜–¾in) layer of fine grit.

Maintenance

Once established, the sink should require little maintenance. In dry spells, it should be watered regularly, especially if it is in full sun. The plants will benefit from an occasional liquid feed to keep them fresh, or a light dressing of bonemeal or organic pellets in spring.

As the plants finish flowering they will benefit from being dead-headed and trimmed lightly to remove any dead or untidy growth.

Prostrate and shrubby alpines can be cut back after flowering to keep them neat, whereas cushion- and hummock-forming alpines merely need dead-heading to keep them tidy.

Phlox douglasii **is ideal if you are new to trough gardening, and 'Rosea' is one of many named forms**

Beginners' alpines

Armeria juniperifolia
Dianthus 'Whatfield Joy'
Gypsophila repens 'Fratensis'
Jovibarba arenaria
Limonium bellidifolium
Phlox douglasii (any named form)
Sempervivum
Sisyrinchium idahoense
Thymus serpyllum 'Minimus'

Some suitable plants for sinks and troughs

These plants are small and neat enough to be contained in a sink. If trailing types are placed at the edges or corners they will cascade over the side and not smother more compact plants.

Helianthemum oelandicum **subsp.** *alpestre* **makes a bright show on the corner of a trough**

More unusual or challenging alpines

Asperula gussonei
Dianthus 'Berlin Snow'
Hypericum oelandicum subsp. *alpestre*
Limonium cosyrense
Minuartia stellata
Origanum 'Buckland'
Silene acaulis 'Mount Snowdon'
Stachys iva
Thymus serpyllum 'Elfin'

Some other containers

In addition to troughs, many other types of container can be used for alpines provided that they have adequate drainage. Smaller containers have the advantage of being easy to move, and they are therefore ideal for plants that need to be switched to different sites during the year.

Saponaria ocymoides **'Snow Tip' tumbles over the edge of a terracotta chimney pot**

Terracotta pots

The natural colour of unglazed terracotta blends well in the garden and weathers over time to give a pleasant aged appearance. Terracotta containers are available in a variety of shapes and range from the cheaper, usually machine-made, shapes to expensive hand-made containers. Unglazed terracotta is ideal for alpines, as moisture can escape through the terracotta itself as well as through the drainage hole. Some terracotta pots, however, are not frost-proof and may crack or flake in very cold conditions. This is usually more of a problem with older containers and very cheap modern designs.

Look for terracotta that has been fired at a very high temperature, as this is more frost-resistant.

Shallow terracotta pans are excellent for small collections of alpines, as they can easily be moved around. We keep our collection of early flowering saxifrages in pans, which we display in the early spring as they come into flower and then move to a cool, shady spot for the summer. Many of our sempervivums are also growing in shallow pans and

A glazed earthenware pot containing *Lewisia cotyledon* **in full bloom**

This wooden planter is filled with an attractive selection of alpines chosen for foliage and flower interest

they are moved around to make displays in different parts of the garden during the hot summer months. Smaller terracotta pots are excellent for individual alpines, particularly those that need to be moved under cover for the winter months. Broken or damaged pots can also look very effective, either laid on their side with the plants spilling out of the broken area or standing up with the compost sloped to display a collection of small alpines.

Glazed earthenware pots also make good alpine containers, although care needs to be taken to avoid those with only a single small drainage hole, which can very quickly become waterlogged in wet weather. Use a layer of broken crocks in the base to help with drainage.

We have found that terracotta and glazed pots standing on hard surfaces, such as concrete or patio slabs, stand a better chance of surviving the winter without cracking if raised off the surface on small pieces of tile or wood. This prevents their filling with water and then freezing solid in cold weather. Never attempt to move a pot when it is frozen, as this increases the risk of damage.

Strawberry pots

These are available in many different shapes and sizes. The best ones for alpines have a slight lip under each of the side pockets. This helps to divert water towards the roots instead of running straight past the plant. Without the lips a large amount of water has to be added to the top of the pot to allow the lower plants to receive any water at all.

Strawberry pots are ideal for displaying collections of plants, especially those needing to grow on a slope such as *Lewisia*. Mixed plantings can also look very attractive, but it is important to choose plants that will not swamp those sitting in the pockets lower down the pot.

Wooden containers

Wooden half-barrels and tubs are readily available in garden centres and nurseries, and these can be used in the same way as troughs or terracotta containers. One disadvantage, however, is that they will not last as long and may need replacing before the plants they contain. Treating them with a wood preservative will help to lengthen their life but care

Home-made shallow wooden planters filled with alpines disguise the top of a disused coal bunker

must be taken to use only products that are recommended for use near plants. Oak barrels can have their life extended by carefully charring the inside with a gas blowlamp to reduce rotting.

You can also make your own wooden planters, and the best timber to use is pressure-treated fencing timber, which should last many years. An advantage of making your own containers is that they can be made to fit particular sites, or to hide eyesores such as manhole covers or coal bunkers.

Hanging baskets

Hanging baskets planted with alpines make wonderful permanent displays that will last many years. Many different types of basket are available, the most popular being made of wire or plastic. Wire baskets need to be lined before planting. We have found that the more durable fibre liners are better than moss, as the moss becomes untidy and falls out after one season. Plastic baskets do not need lining, but they can only be planted on the top, making it difficult to hide the basket itself. Some plastic baskets have water reservoirs, and these should be removed when planting up with alpines in order to prevent the compost remaining waterlogged in wet weather.

More unusual containers

As well as the more traditional containers, alpines can be grown in almost any receptacle provided that it has some form of drainage to prevent the compost becoming waterlogged. We have successfully used old drainage pipes, hollow concrete blocks and tin baths. Hollow sections of tree trunks look particularly effective placed in the full sun and planted with a collection of *Sempervivum*.

Planting containers

The method of planting containers is similar to that for troughs. The container should be filled with the same three layers, starting with a drainage layer of gravel or finely broken crocks – in deep containers this can be up to a quarter of the depth. The compost layer should consist of the same mix as for a trough, with similar adjustments made to suit the plants being grown. The container should be filled to within 5cm (2in) of the top of the container. The actual planting should be done in the same way as for a trough, and then the compost top-dressed with a material to suit the container. After planting, water the container thoroughly to firm the compost around the plants and settle everything in.

The new compost in the container should provide the plants with sufficient feed for their first season. Subsequently they will need feeding each spring with a long-lasting solid feed such as pelleted poultry manure, or regular feeding during the year with a dilute solution of tomato feed.

Once established, alpines in containers should need little maintenance apart from trimming after flowering and perhaps in the early spring. They should be watered regularly in dry weather. During the winter or very wet spells they may benefit from being moved under cover to prevent them becoming too waterlogged.

Planting hanging baskets

As hanging baskets will dry out more quickly than other containers, the compost mix should be adjusted to hold more water. We have found that a mix of John Innes No. 2 and good peat-based compost in equal proportions is ideal – the basket should not be too heavy to hang easily. A good idea with a wire basket is to sink a small flower pot into the compost before planting: if you pour water into this pot, the water will soak into the compost rather than run through the wire sides.

Alpine baskets will provide a succession of flower and foliage interest throughout the year, and while they will not give the spectacular display of traditional basket schemes they will last much longer, and the plants will stand up to periods of bad weather without being damaged.

Alpine baskets should be fed with a dilute solution of tomato feed every three or four weeks during the spring and summer. Once each plant has finished flowering it should be trimmed back neatly to allow the other plants to develop. In the early spring the plants should be trimmed back hard and the basket top dressed with fresh compost.

Geranium, Dianthus, Parahebe **and** *Sedum* **are among the alpines in this hanging basket**

A selection of alpines for a hanging basket

These are all sturdy, robust plants that will provide a long succession of flowering, with the foliage of some remaining evergreen to maintain some interest over winter.

Dianthus 'Dewdrop'
Geranium sanguineum var. *striatum*
Gypsophila repens 'Dubia'
Helianthemum 'Ben Ledi'
Parahebe catarractae 'Delight'
Persicaria vaccinifolia
Sedum spurium var. *album*
Thymus serpyllum 'Russetings'
Veronica pectinata

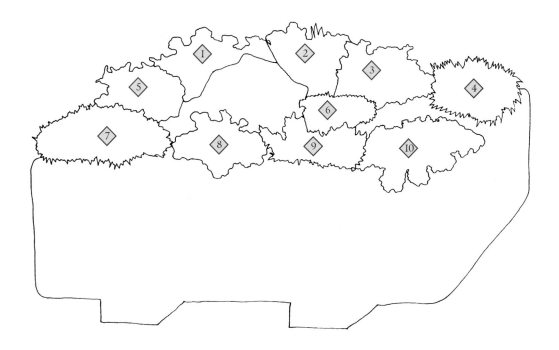

Plants

① *Alyssum spinosum* 'Roseum'

② *Sisyrinchium idahoense* 'Album'

③ *Geranium dalmaticum*

④ *Phlox douglasii* 'Red Admiral'

⑤ *Limonium minutum*

⑥ *Sempervivum* 'Corsair'

⑦ *Dianthus* 'Berlin Snow'

⑧ *Erodium* × *variabile* 'Flore Pleno'

⑨ *Veronica prostrata* 'Nana'

⑩ *Asperula gussonei*

Trough design *Illustrated in early summer* **Stone trough 50 × 35cm (20 × 14in)**

Alpine pan

Illustrated in early summer **38cm (15in) diameter earthenware low pan**

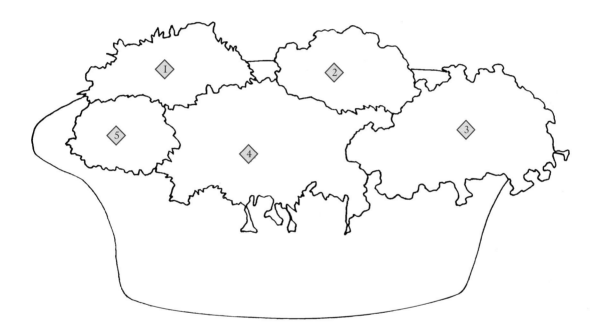

Plants

① *Dianthus* 'Whatfield Wisp'

② *Dianthus* 'La Bourboule'

③ *Dianthus* 'Nyewood's Cream'

④ *Dianthus petraeus* subsp. *noeanus*

⑤ *Dianthus alpinus* 'Joan's Blood'

CHAPTER SEVEN

OTHER WAYS OF GROWING ALPINES

Gravel areas

Areas of gravel, particularly on light well-drained soils, are ideal for planting a wide selection of alpines. Gravel areas can be any size and shape and are ideal to fit into awkward-shaped spaces, although to be successful they should be sited in an open sunny position. A wide range of gravels and chippings can be used to cover the area.
In regions where rocks form part of the landscape, chippings from the native rock will blend in well, but in other areas water-washed gravels may well look more effective. Large areas often benefit from the addition of a few rocks to break up the flat surface, although care is needed in placing these. A small group of two or three larger rocks is more effective than a scattering of individual ones.

Preparing the bed

As with other alpine features, time spent preparing the gravel bed will be repaid with a long-lasting, low-maintenance feature. Before beginning any

Left A small front garden, transformed into a gravel bed with tufa rock and filled with alpines to provide colour and interest all year

The smallest areas are suitable for gravel plantings – here, a narrow strip between house and path is planted with sempervivums and *Saxifraga*

construction work you should clear the area of all perennial weeds, using a systemic weedkiller such as glyphosate if necessary. Once the site is clear, the most important step is to ensure good drainage. On light soils, all that is usually needed is to dig the soil to remove any compaction. If you have a heavy clay soil, then siting the bed on a slight slope where the water can run off is a good idea, but even on a slope the addition of land drainage pipes will greatly increase the range of plants that can be grown. Drainage pipes should be laid in a herringbone pattern leading to a ditch or suitable drain. The pipes should be laid about 30cm (12in) deep and 60–90cm (2–3ft) apart. If funds permit, backfilling the trenches with gravel will ensure that the water drains away rapidly. Digging a quantity of coarse grit into the soil will benefit most soils, allowing the water to drain more freely from the surface.

Once the ground has been prepared, it is a good idea to cover the area with a weed control membrane. There are several different types on the market, though in our experience the woven black plastic types are more durable and easier to work with than the spun fibre products. The membrane will restrict the growth of any remaining weeds and will also prevent the soil and gravel layers mixing over time.

With the fabric in place, the plants can be laid out on the surface and moved around until the desired effect is achieved. Once you are satisfied with the arrangement, you can begin planting.

Planting a gravel bed

We have excellent results in planting gravel beds using the following method:

1   Cut a cross in the fabric slightly larger than the base of the pot (if you make the cut at 45 degrees to the weave the fabric will not fray).

2   Fold back the fabric and loosen the soil beneath with a trowel.

3   Using a sharp knife, carefully cut out the bottom of the pot.

4   Place the bottomless pot onto the surface of the loosened soil, firming it in gently. The pot should remain about 7–10cm (3–4in) above the surface of the fabric.

5   Once all the plants have been put in place, carefully cover the whole area with a layer of your chosen gravel, deep enough to cover the pots, and leave the plants' foliage on the surface. The foliage may need to be carefully lifted to allow the gravel to be placed underneath.

6   After planting, carefully water the whole area to settle the gravel and wash any fine particles from the foliage.

This method allows the roots of the plants to grow out and travel downwards from the pot into the soil, while making it easier to plant and arrange gravel around them.

Maintenance of gravel beds

An established gravel bed will need little maintenance apart from the routine trimming and tidying of the plants as they finish flowering. Many alpines will seed readily into the gravel, which provides ideal germination conditions, and the growth of the resultant seedlings does need to be controlled or they will swamp the bed. The easiest method of control is to dead-head the plants as they finish flowering to prevent them shedding their seed. If you want to let some seeds develop they can easily be controlled by lightly raking through the unwanted seedlings with a hand trowel. Do this on a hot sunny day and the disturbed seedlings will shrivel and die very quickly. This method is also a very effective way to control any weed seedlings that do emerge.

This gravel area in front of a border contains low-growing alpines and incorporates old chimney pots planted with alpines

Gravel beds usually require very little watering once they are established. The thick layer of gravel keeps the soil beneath moist in all but the most prolonged dry spells. The roots of the plants travel deep into the soil in search of water, so they are less dependent on further watering.

The plants in the bed will benefit from the application of a slow-release feed each spring. We prefer to use pelleted poultry manure, but any balanced feed can be used provided that care is taken to prevent it scorching the delicate plant foliage.

Plant selection

Gravel areas are suitable for many different alpines that enjoy hot, sunny conditions. A range of different effects can be produced by carefully selecting the plants. A collection of low-growing plants can be used to create an alpine lawn, full of colour and leaving very little gravel exposed. A more varied effect can be achieved by incorporating dwarf shrubs and conifers with groups of mixed alpines, separated by areas of gravel to contrast with the foliage of the plants.

Thymus, Iris **and** *Dianthus* **are excellent for gravel beds**

Add one or more troughs or containers of alpines if you wish. You can also incorporate other features in a large gravel area, such as stepping stones or a seat.

Excellent plants for hot, sunny gravel beds include *Tanacetum densum* subsp. *amani*, *Achillea*, *Scabiosa*, *Veronica*, *Hypericum*, *Helianthemum*, *Sempervivum* and *Scutellaria*.

Around ponds

Alpines grown around a pond can provide a link to larger scale surrounding plantings, softening the pond and allowing light to reach the water. Rocks are often incorporated into the surroundings of ponds and waterfalls, and pockets created between these can provide excellent planting positions for alpines. Care must be taken to ensure that the pockets are free-draining and do not become waterlogged at the base, and they should also be positioned so that spray from a fountain or waterfall does not reach the foliage of the plants. You can also leave gaps for low planting in paved areas around ponds.

Veronica prostrata **'Mrs Holt' thrives in a sunny gravel bed**

Erodium × *variabile* **'Bishop's Form'** and *Achillea* **'Huteri'** **make attractive mounds by the side of this pond**

Plant selection

Trailing alpines such as *Frankenia, Gypsophila* and *Veronica* are very effective at providing a softening effect to hard rocks. They should be kept trimmed to prevent them reaching the water, and a trim in the early autumn will prevent the leaves falling into the water. Mound-forming alpines have a softening effect on paved edges.

Around waterfalls and other damp areas, use moisture-loving alpines such as *Calceolaria, Dodecatheon* and *Primula*, as these will thrive in moist, but not waterlogged, pockets and crevices.

Paving and patios

Areas of stone paving can often look very stark, so planting low-growing alpines into pockets between the paving softens the overall effect, and with careful plant selection this will provide additional colour and interest throughout the year. Robust varieties that grow as low mounds or mats, such as *Achillea, Erodium* and *Thymus,* will tolerate being trodden on occasionally

Right **A path can be made more interesting with a few alpines planted into gaps**

Below **A golden thyme and** *Hypericum reptans* **add colour in these paving pockets**

with no ill effects and can be planted in areas that are frequently walked over. Varieties with more delicate foliage, such as *Diascia* and *Papaver*, can be planted in corners or areas that are not walked over regularly.

An ideal beginners' selection could include *Achillea* 'Huteri', *Campanula garganica, Thymus serpyllum* 'Goldstream' and *Veronica prostrata*.

It is possible to plant into any patio or paving area provided there is soil beneath the stones. The stones themselves will allow water to drain away from the base of the plant and, once established, the plant should find all the moisture it needs in the cool earth beneath the stones or slabs.

This type of planting looks very effective in large areas, such as a brick or paved patio, but it can also be worthwhile on a small scale, perhaps just in a small patch outside a door in order to hide the hard lines of slabs or paving bricks.

Planting into a patio

1 Create a suitable pocket. This needs to be only just bigger than a pot in diameter. If you are building a new area, the easiest option is simply to leave out a few small pavers or pieces of stone (we usually leave out the odd-shaped pieces that are difficult to cut!). With existing areas you need carefully to remove small pieces of the surface and clear away any hardcore beneath.

2 Remove any layers of sand or hardcore from the bottom of the pocket and loosen the existing soil at the base of the hole.

3 Fill the pocket with gritty alpine compost (equal proportions of John Innes No. 2, peat-based compost and flint grit).

4 Ensure that your plants are all moist. If the compost is dry, soak them in a shallow bucket of water until the compost is thoroughly moistened.

5 Before planting, stand your plants out in their pots on the pockets and move them around until you are satisfied with the arrangement.

6 Remove each plant from its pot. Dig a hole in its chosen pocket slightly larger than the pot and deep enough so that the crown of the plant will be level with or slightly above the surface of the paving stones.

7 Place the plant into the hole, firming it gently into the compost at the base. Carefully fill the hole around the plant with compost, firming it in gently and taking care to keep the crown of the plant level with or slightly above the stone surface.

8 Water the plants in well to settle the compost around the roots.

9 Top dress the compost around the plant with a suitable gravel or grit to match the paving.

Until they are established the plants should be watered regularly, particularly during hot, dry spells, but once they begin to grow away well watering should be stopped to encourage them to produce a strong root system beneath the paving. Feeding is not usually necessary unless the underlying soil is very poor or a large number of plants are used in a small area. If the plants begin to look tired, a careful application of a slow-release feed such as pelleted poultry manure can be made around each pocket in the spring or early autumn.

Saxifraga × *urbium* **newly planted into a paving pocket – the compost can be top dressed with gravel or grit**

Cracks in paving

The cracks between old flagstones or on areas of crazy paving need to be regularly maintained to keep them free from weeds and moss. An attractive alternative is to plant them with creeping alpines that will run around, under and in between the stones and fill the gaps with attractive flowers and foliage – swamping small weed seedlings and reducing the maintenance required. The best plants to use for this are some of the more invasive spreading alpines with running shoots that root as they spread, such as *Leptinella potentillina, Oxalis magellanica* and *Pratia*. These can be a problem planted in open beds, but controlled by the paving they become a very colourful feature. By using young plants or breaking up larger ones we have had success establishing plants in gaps as narrow as 1–2cm (½–1in).

Planting into cracks

1 Using a narrow trowel or an old kitchen knife, clean the old soil, moss and rubbish out of the cracks to a depth of about 4–5cm (1½–2in), or deeper if the crack is wide enough.
2 Before starting to plant, make sure that the plants are moist in their pots, soaking them if necessary.
3 If you are using young plants, carefully tease the compost away from the roots to leave a rootball small enough to fit into the cracks without being too compressed.
4 If you are using larger plants of spreading varieties, each potful can usually be cut into sections small enough to fit into the cracks by using an old knife. With this method, a plant in a 7cm (3in) square pot can often be cut to produce six or seven small clumps for planting.

5 Place each plant into a crack, spreading the roots out as much as possible. Backfill around the plant using a dry compost to allow it to flow into the spaces surrounding the roots (John Innes compost is ideal for this).
6 When planting is complete, water the whole area thoroughly to allow the soil to settle into the cracks.
7 When the paving is dry, top up any cracks where the soil has sunk and then water the area again.

Young plants and clumps of plant should be watered regularly until they are established, particularly on sunny days, but once they begin to show signs of growth, watering should be gradually reduced to encourage them to produce a strong root system beneath the paving.

Steps

Alpines can be used to soften the hard surfaces of steps in the same way as patios. They are particularly effective at hiding the edges of steps to help blend them in with surrounding plantings. Cracked and damaged areas at the edges of steps can be hidden by careful planting, avoiding the need for expensive repairs and adding additional interest to the feature. New flights of steps can have planting pockets incorporated in the sides and at the base.

Your choice of plants is important: trailing and spreading varieties, for instance, should be used with care and only where they can be kept well away from any area where they might get tangled in people's feet. Brightly coloured alpines such as *Helianthemum* could be used at the ends of the treads, particularly where these need to be clearly visible.

Walls

Walls can be constructed in many different ways, and they provide excellent growing conditions for alpines. Both old and new walls can be planted with alpines, particularly species that prefer to grow on a vertical face (for example, *Lewisia*), allowing water to drain away rapidly. Whatever the age or type of wall, soil needs to be available for the roots to grow and anchor the plants. Some plants will grow with only a tiny amount of soil, but most require a good depth. In single old walls, uneven surfaces tend to fill up with debris and organic matter over the years, creating a base for small plants to grow in. In new walls, you need to create planting holes or crevices.

Retaining walls

If pockets can be made in the brick or stonework these make excellent planting sites. The vertical face provides near perfect drainage, and the soil behind the wall will remain cool and moist even in the hottest weather. On south-facing walls try plants such as *Asperula gussonei*, *Parahebe lyalli*, *Pterocephalus perennis*, or *Saponaria ocymoides*. On a west- or east-facing wall *Lewisia cotyledon* hybrids will look spectacular, while on a north wall try *Campanula* 'Birch Hybrid' or *Saxifraga*. Once established, alpines such as *Erinus alpinus* will seed themselves into cracks and crevices in walls.

To plant into a vertical wall, remove just enough soil to accommodate the rootball, firm the plant gently into the hole and then carefully backfill using a moist compost so that it does not run out of the hole. After planting, water each alpine individually with a fine spout on a watering can to prevent the soil washing from the hole. Continue this careful watering until the plants become established.

Double walls

If the gap between the walls is filled with soil the wall can be treated as a very narrow raised bed (see Chapter 5) and planted according to its aspect. You can plant into the top and also into the sides by making holes or crevices through to the soil in the centre. If the wall was built without a soil core, then it will be necessary to create pockets of soil wherever possible along the top, and care must be taken to ensure these are able to drain freely to prevent the plants becoming waterlogged. With limited soil, planting choice is more restricted. For hot sunny walls, choose plants such as *Sempervivum* and *Sedum*, which will establish in the soil pockets and then gradually spread out over the rest of the wall. In shadier positions try *Chiastophyllum*, *Saxifraga* or *Viola*.

Borders

Many alpines are robust enough to use in well-drained soil, either in small, narrow borders or at the edges of larger beds and borders.

The small scale of most alpines makes them ideal for the narrow strips of soil between adjacent gardens, or alongside the paths and driveways that are often a feature of modern housing estates. By using alpines together with miniature conifers and dwarf shrubs, the limited space can be planted with a variety of plants to provide interest through the year. Alpines such as *Armeria*, *Aubrieta* and shrubby *Thymus* can be planted along the edges of concrete paths and driveways to soften the straight lines without spreading too far and becoming an obstruction.

In larger borders alpines can provide a low edging, spilling over and creating a softening effect that helps to blend the bed into a

Mounds of *Thymus* **'Porlock' and** *Armeria maritima* **spill out from a narrow border over the edge of this concrete driveway**

surrounding path or paving area. Many robust low-growing alpines, such as *Achillea* 'Huteri', *Campanula poscharskyana* and *Geranium sanguinuem*, also make effective ground cover, especially under a planting of open shrubs such as roses.

Clumps of alpines at the front of a border can be used to provide additional splashes of colour. Sedums, prostrate thymes and *Potentilla* × *tonguei* make colourful carpets at the front of a sunny border. The bright yellow flowers of *Chiastophyllum oppositifolium* make a stunning display at the front of a shady border, while the bright orange-red flowers of *Penstemon pinifolius* 'Wisley Flame' add fire to the front of a sunny bed.

Right **Pasque flowers are excellent at the front of borders where you can enjoy them in spring – this is** *Pulsatilla vulgaris* **'Eva Constance'**

Campanula **'Birch Hybrid' and a creeping thyme make a splash of colour between a path and the plants behind them**

A top dressing of grit around alpines planted in borders helps to keep their necks and foliage dry

While some robust alpines will grow in all but the heaviest soils, they will be happier if the soil is improved before planting. The easiest way to do this is to introduce grit or coarse sand. This should be dug into as much of the bed as possible so that you do not create a series of small pockets which then collect the water from the surrounding soil. Once the soil has been improved, the plants can be put in as described in Chapter 3. If the whole bed is not going to be top dressed it is a good idea to put a handful of grit around the crown of each alpine to keep it off the soil while the plant becomes established. Water the plants in well after planting, and continue regular watering until they are well established.

Plant selection and colour schemes

Here are a few ideas to start with: by using the plant descriptions in the next chapter, you will be able to put many more colour schemes together.

✳ An ideal beginner's selection of alpines for the front of a border would be *Iberis sempervirens* 'Schneeflocke', *Geranium sanguineum* var. *striatum*, *Sedum kamtschaticum* var. *floriferum* 'Weihenstephaner Gold', *Campanula poscharskyana* and *Armeria maritima* 'Splendens'. These are all reliable, robust alpines providing a long season of colour.

Armeria maritima **'Splendens' is a stunning but reliable alpine for border edges**

✳ Use *Geranium sanguineum* var. *striatum,*
Helianthemum 'Ben Ledi' and *Parahebe lyallii*
'Julie-Anne', with their flower colours of
pink, rose-red and white, in front of shrub
roses or similar-coloured herbaceous
perennials.

✳ A front border planting of *Armeria maritima*
'Vindictive', *Campanula poscharskyana* 'Stella' and
Veronica austriaca subsp. *teucrium* 'Royal Blue',
with flowers of rich pink, deep violet and
deep blue, provides strong colour for impact.
They will form good mats of foliage, together
with many flowers.

Paving area *Illustrated in early-mid summer*

Plants

1   *Helianthemum* 'Sterntaler'

2   *Chaenorhinum origanifolium*

3   *Thymus serpyllum* 'Russetings'

4   *Papaver alpinum*

5   *Thymus* 'Doone Valley'

6   *Campanula garganica*

7   *Veronica prostrata*

8   *Bellium minutum*

Border edge (small length of) *Illustrated in late summer*

Plants

1. *Berberis thunbergii* 'Dart's Red Lady'
2. *Potentilla fruticosa* 'Abbotswood'
3. *Campanula persicifolia* 'Chettle Charm'
4. *Stipa tenuissima*
5. *Spiraea betulifolia* var. *aemiliana*
6. *Hebe* 'Heidi'
7. *Veronica spicata* 'Alba'
8. *Aster novi-belgii* 'Jenny'
9. *Lavandula angustifolia* 'Imperial Gem'
10. *Pulsatilla vulgaris*
11. *Scutellaria alpina*
12. *Sedum kamtschaticum* var. *floriferum* 'Weihenstephaner Gold'
13. *Sedum* 'Ruby Glow'
14. *Helianthemum* 'Sudbury Gem'
15. *Parahebe lyallii* 'Julie-Anne'
16. *Geranium cinereum* 'Laurence Flatman'
17. *Dianthus* 'Dewdrop'

CHAPTER EIGHT

PLANT DESCRIPTIONS

All the plants mentioned throughout this book are described here in more detail, together with further examples of species and cultivars where appropriate.

For each plant we have indicated which position they prefer (sun, shade), whether they need sharp, good or ordinary drainage or moisture-retentive soil, and their flowering season. Dimensions given are height × spread.

Position

☀ sun   ☼ semi-shade   ● shade

Flowering season

❀ Spring   ❀ Summer   ❀ Autumn   ❀ Winter

Drainage

|◖◖◖| moisture-retentive |◖◖| ordinary drainage |◖| good drainage | | sharp drainage

Achillea

☀ |◖| | | | ❀ ❀ ❀ | | | |

Long-flowering alpines with ferny foliage and flat heads composed of many little flowers. *A.* 'Huteri' (8 × 20–30cm; 3 × 8–12in) is a neat hummock of aromatic, deeply cut grey leaves, with pure white flowers. *A.* × *lewisii* 'King Edward' (10 × 23cm; 4 × 9in) has greyish-green leaves and very attractive, soft, lemon-yellow flowers. A larger species is *A. chrysocoma*, with densely hairy, aromatic leaves topped by 15–25cm (6–10in) stems of bright yellow flowers. This makes a spreading mat of 30cm (12in) or more, ideal for front of border or gravel garden.

Achillea **'Huteri'**

Acinos alpinus

A pretty plant forming tufts of slender, spreading shoots covered in neat, oval leaves, reaching 15cm (6in) high × 25cm (10in) across. It carries numerous leafy spikes of small, reddish-violet lipped flowers with white markings. Cut back hard after flowering. Very easy from seed.

Acinos alpinus

Aethionema armenum

Aethionema

These little semi-evergreen shrublets, easily grown from seed, have somewhat succulent leaves, and rounded heads of flowers borne at the ends of shoots. They can be short-lived if the soil is not really well drained, but produce masses of seed. *A. armenum* is compact and ideal for troughs, reaching 10 × 10cm (4 × 4in), with blue-grey leaves and abundant clusters of pink flowers. *A. grandiflorum* is taller, to 30cm (12in) with blue-green leaves and many large rose-pink flowers in dense clusters. *A.* 'Warley Rose' (15 × 15cm; 6 × 6in) is a widely grown hybrid with lovely deep pink flowers.

Alchemilla

☀ ☀ 💧 | | | ✿ ✿ | | | | |

The main attraction of Lady's Mantles is their soft, velvety, lobed leaves, though the sprays of tiny yellowish-green flowers borne profusely in summer are also pretty. The tufts of leaves form low carpets, tolerant of partial shade. *A. alpina* (15 × 30cm; 6 × 12in) has deep green leaves, silvery beneath, and pale greenish-yellow flowers. *A. erythropoda* (15 × 20cm; 6 × 8in) is very attractive and neat with soft, wavy-edged leaves and tiny lime green flowers that redden with age. *A. ellenbeckii* is unusual in having trailing red stems with small, deeply cleft leaves, good for ground cover, spreading up to 30cm (12in) but only 5cm (2in) high.

Alchemilla erythropoda

Alyssum serpyllifolium

Alyssum spinosum '**Roseum**'

Alyssum

☀ ⊔ | | | ✿ ✿ | | | | |

A. spinosum 'Roseum' is a dense, spiny shrublet 10cm (4in) high, with soft, rose-pink flowers; *A. serpyllifolium* (10cm; 4in) is a trailing species with golden heads of flowers. Both have tiny silvery leaves and are ideal for troughs or raised beds. They can be raised from seed.

Anacyclus

☀ ⊔ | | | ✿ ✿ ✿ | | | |

The Mount Atlas Daisy, *A. pyrethrum* var. *depressus* (8 × 15cm; 3 × 6in), forms a completely prostrate rosette of finely cut, greyish-green leaves. The numerous white daisy-like flowers are borne on radiating horizontal stems, and the petals are crimson on the reverse, particularly noticeable when the flowers close at night. In a gritty, sharply drained spot, it readily self-seeds.

Androsace

There are many species of rock jasmines, forming cushions or mats composed of tight rosettes, and though several are best in the alpine house, several can successfully be grown outside. The flowers have a distinct central eye, and are borne on stalks in the centre of the rosettes. *A. carnea* (5 × 5cm; 2 × 2in) has stiff, pointed leaves and pink flowers, and subsp. *laggeri* has magenta flowers. *A. lanuginosa* (4 × 18cm; 1½ × 7in) has showy clusters of lilac-pink flowers in rounded heads during mid-summer and trailing stems of hairy green leaves growing from the main rosettes and forming a mat. *A. sempervivoides* (up to 7 × 30cm; 3 × 12in) has leathery leaves, the rosettes spreading to form wide mats, and pink yellow-eyed flowers.

Anemone

There are several small, showy, easily grown anemones, with tufts of deeply cut leaves and cup-shaped flowers. *A. caroliniana*, ideal for gravel areas and raised beds, has pretty cream flowers on 15–20cm (6–8in) stems, produced in summer and often again in autumn. The long-lasting seed-heads are also attractive, eventually releasing clouds of fluffy seeds. *A. sylvestris*, the snowdrop anemone, has fragrant, slightly drooping white flowers on 30cm (12in) stems in mid-spring, preferring a cooler position. *A. × lesseri* (30cm; 12in) is very colourful, with bright, deep pink flowers that have a darker eye. *A. nemerosa*, the Wood Anemone, has lobed, toothed leaves on running stems (15 × 30cm; 6 × 12in), and white flowers tinted mauve. There are several forms, including 'Vestal' (pure white) and 'Robinsoniana' (pale lavender blue).

Antennaria

The species commonly grown form dense, close-knit mats of small leaves, eventually making attractive ground cover, which you can grow dwarf bulbs through or use among paving or to edge a small border. *A. microphylla* has green leaves with a silvery, woolly coating and short stems of rose-pink, fluffy flowers, while *A. parvifolia* is more silvery with whitish fluffy flowers. They are both prostrate, with 5–10cm (2–4in) flower stems, and can be increased by division once established.

Anemone caroliniana

Anthemis marschalliana

This makes a neat mound of beautiful, finely cut, silver foliage, with large, deep golden-yellow, daisy-like flowers, and is lovely for a dry, gritty soil. Reaching 15–20cm (6–8in) by 20cm (8in), it is easily divided by removing rooted pieces.

Antirrhinum sempervirens

An attractive little plant, 5 × 20cm (2 × 8in), with semi-prostrate, tangled stems covered in sticky hairs and bearing quite thick, oval, green leaves. Small white snapdragon flowers, marked yellow and purple, are carried in abundance. Grows readily from seed or cuttings.

Aquilegia

With their distinctive neat, lobed foliage of green or bluish-green and nodding, spurred flowers, the dwarf columbines include several worthwhile species. A. flabellata 'Ministar' (15cm; 6in) has sturdy blue-mauve and white flowers above glaucous foliage, A. bertolonii (15cm; 6in) has dark green leaves and violet-blue flowers, A. laramiensis is a tiny gem of 5–8cm (2–3in) with little creamy white flowers. These are suitable for troughs and raised beds, and will perpetuate themselves by self-seeding, though they will also hybridise extremely readily.

Arabis

A. alpina subsp. caucasica has several popular cultivars, such as 'Rosea', 'Flore Pleno' and 'Pink Pearl', that provide masses of spring colour, covering walls with their spreading rosettes of leaves and white or pink flowers. They generally grow to 15 × 25cm (6 × 10in) or more. A. ferdinandi-coburgii 'Old Gold' is neater, forming flattish mats of shining green and gold foliage, with 10cm (4in) stems of white flowers very early in spring. The form 'Variegata' has green and ivory leaves, tinged red in winter.

Arenaria

Small-leafed alpines with starry flowers, forming cushions or trailing mats. A. montana has long trailing stems of deep green foliage, ideal for cascading down walls or forming a carpet. Reaching 5cm × 15–20cm (2 × 6–8in), it carries masses of rounded, pure white flowers. A. purpurascens (2 × 10cm; ¾ × 4in) is a pretty species with short-stemmed, pale pinkish-mauve flowers covering the low cushions of small, pointed leaves. A. tetraquetra is a dense cushion of tiny, closely packed, triangular leaves studded in summer with solitary white flowers. It is excellent for a trough, growing to 2.5cm × 10–15cm (1 × 4–6in).

Armeria juniperifolia **'Alba'**

Armeria

☀ ⬦ | ❋ ❋ ❋ ❋ | | | | | |

The alpine thrifts have dense tufts of linear leaves and globular heads of papery flowers borne in succession over summer and sometimes in autumn. *A. maritima* is well known, with mounds of dark green grassy leaves that can spread to form good ground cover. There are many named forms, with flowers on 15–25cm (6–10in) stems, including 'Alba', with large white flowers; 'Splendens' (deep rosy pink); 'Vindictive' (reddish-pink/rich rose pink); 'Düsseldorfer Stolz' (rich crimson). These are lovely in gravel areas and borders, the foliage clumps remaining evergreen throughout the year. A smaller, neat species for troughs and raised beds is *A. juniperifolia* (2–5 × 10–15cm; ¾–2 × 4–6in), with tight hummocks of tiny needle-like leaves and little heads of pale pink thrift flowers in early summer. 'Bevan's Variety' is deep rose pink, 'Beechwood' is bright pink and 'Alba' is white.

Armeria maritima **'Splendens'**

Arenaria purpurascens

Artemisia

☀ ⬜ | | | ❋ ❋ | | | | |

Beautiful silvery foliage plants with greyish flower heads, forming low mounds that add valuable foliage interest to alpine plantings. *A. schmidtiana* 'Nana' (8 × 20–30cm; 3 × 8–12in) has silky, finely cut, silver foliage, eventually spreading into a low mat. It is effective at the front of a border and lovely with dwarf bulbs growing through it. *A. caucasica* subsp. *caucasica* (5 × 15cm; 2 × 6in) is a slow-growing, bright silver cushion of fine, feathery foliage, small enough for troughs. Trim artemisias in spring to encourage new growth and reduce woodiness.

Aruncus aethusifolius

A lovely diminutive form of Goat's Beard, with 20cm (8in) tufts of finely divided ferny foliage that is fresh green in summer and turns to red and bronze shades during autumn before falling. The little pokers of white foamy flowers are borne on 20–30cm (8–12in) reddish stems. Easily grown from seed, and can be divided once established.

Asperula

Two species worthy of planting in a trough or raised bed are *A. gussonei* and *A. lilaciflora* subsp. *lilaciflora*, both reaching 5 × 10–15cm (2 × 4–6in).
The latter forms a low, prostrate mat of tiny leaves with deep pink flowers, while *A. gussonei* has dense, compact tufts of tiny needle-like dark green leaves, studded with small, stemless flesh-pink flowers, and requires gritty soil.

Asperula lilaciflora **subsp.** *lilaciflora*

Aster alpinus

With its low tufts composed of leafy basal rosettes, and solitary, relatively large, daisy-like flower heads, this is an easy going, neat alpine for a sunny spot, reaching 15–20cm (6–8in) × up to 20cm (8in). It usually has mauve or purple flowers, always with a yellow centre, though pink and white forms are also available. 'Trimix' is a seed-raised strain composed of a mixture of white, mauve and pink flowers, and 'Pinkie' has flowers in shades of pink.

Aster alpinus '**Trimix**'

Aubrieta

A well-loved plant, clothing countless walls in spring with masses of flowers in shades of mauve, purple and red. There are numerous hybrids (5–10 × 20–30cm; 2–4 × 8–12in or more) that are widely grown, with grey-green foliage that will trail or form carpets. Cut back hard after flowering to tidy and promote fresh growth. Strains such as 'Royal Red' and 'Royal Violet' can be raised from seed, though some variation in colour will occur. Named forms, such as 'Aureovariegata' (yellow and green variegated leaves and pale mauve flowers), 'Alix Brett' (double carmine) and 'Doctor Mules' (violet blue) must be propagated from cuttings.

Aurinia saxatilis

Known as Gold Dust, this forms a mound 20cm (8in) high, often spreading much wider, and is covered in showy bright yellow flowers. There are various named forms, some more compact, including 'Goldkugel' (rich golden yellow), 'Citrina' (pale lemon) and 'Dudley Nevill' (orange buff). Frequently seen spilling over walls and banks, providing plenty of spring colour.

Bellium minutum

This makes a completely prostrate mat of tiny, rounded leaves, rooting down as it spreads, so it is wonderful for growing among paving or as a patch on a gravel or raised bed. In a dryish, sunny spot, it can be covered for weeks in little, white, red-backed daisy-like flowers on 3cm (1in) stems.

Calceolaria

There are some hardy species suitable for a peat bed or any cool, moist soil rich in humus, with their distinctive pouched flowers, the lower lip inflated. *C.* 'John Innes' has rosettes of hairy leaves, spreading to 25cm (10in), and 15–18cm (6–7in) stems of large, bright yellow flowers, while *C. polyrrhiza* (3 × 15cm; 1 × 6in) has running shoots and yellow flowers marked purple. *C. tenella* (5cm; 2in) is a pretty species whose creeping stems form a tight mat, clothed in small, rounded leaves and bearing tiny, yellow pouched flowers. All may be increased by division.

Campanula

☀ ☼ 〚◊◊〛 | | | ✳ ✳ ✳ | | | | |

A large genus containing many delightful alpine types with flowers in various shades of blue and mauve, and white. *C. carpatica* (10 × 10cm; 4 × 4in) has large upturned bell-shaped flowers over bright green mounds of long-stalked foliage, and the numerous named forms include 'Blaue Clips' (china blue) and 'Chewton Joy' (pale lavender). *C.* 'Birch Hybrid' (10cm × 15–20cm; 4 × 6–8in) is a leafy, robust, free flowering plant with mauve bells giving a long-lasting show. *C.* 'Hallii' (6 × 10cm; 2½ × 4in) forms dainty tufts of light green leaves and carries masses of small, white hanging bells. *C. cochleariifolia* (7–10cm × 15cm; 3–4in × 6in or more) has tufts of tiny heart-shaped leaves with many blue hanging bells, and the form 'Elizabeth Oliver' is very dainty with fully double flowers of soft powder blue. *C. garganica*, easily raised from seed, has tufts of little, long-stalked, ivy-shaped leaves, and graceful sprays of starry blue flowers. It reaches 10 × 15cm (4 × 6in), while the form 'Blue Diamond' is slightly larger,

with downy, greyish-green leaves and deep blue flowers. 'Dickson's Gold' makes a splash of colour in a partially shaded spot, with its golden leaves and blue flowers. *C. pulla* (7–10 × 15cm; 3–4 × 6in) has slender, hanging bells of a rich, deep violet, held just above its carpet of glossy oval leaves, and requires a rich soil with lime, and partial shade. *C. poscharskyana* (15–20 × 30cm; 6–8 × 12in or more) makes excellent ground cover or will trail over walls, banks and containers, forming a thick, spreading mat of leaves with a long succession of starry lavender-blue flowers in clusters. Named forms include 'E.H. Frost' (pale green foliage, milk-white flowers tinted blue); 'Stella' (compact with deep violet flowers over dark green leaves); and 'Lisduggan Variety' (slow-growing, with lavender-pink flowers). All are long flowering, often well into autumn. Named forms of *Campanula* can be propagated by cuttings or division; species by seed, which is very tiny.

Campanula cochleariifolia **'Elizabeth Oliver'**

Chaenorhinum origanifolium

Chaenorhinum origanifolium

A pretty alpine with leafy stems carrying lipped and spurred flowers, coloured rich purple with a paler throat. Growing up to 20cm (8in), it will give weeks of colour in a raised bed, wall or container. It self-seeds easily, forming colonies particularly in well-drained, gritty soil. 'Blue Dream' has flowers of bluish-mauve.

Chiastophyllum oppositifolium

This has fleshy, toothed leaves on thick stems, and very attractive, pendent sprays of yellow, starry flowers, looking very much like dangling catkins. A patch of this in a peat bed or cool position in soil that doesn't dry out is an eye-catching sight in full flower. 'Jim's Pride' has bold, green and white variegated leaves that become markedly pink-tinged in winter, and produces arching stems of bright lemon yellow-flowers. Both grow to 15 × 15–20cm (6 × 6–8in). Propagate by cuttings in early summer.

Chiastophyllum oppositifolium

Convolvulus lineatus

An extremely attractive tufted plant making neat mats of linear, silky-haired, silvery leaves. Pure white or pink-tinged funnel-shaped flowers are borne over many weeks, opening up in the sun, and are very showy. It is hardy in very gritty, well-drained soil in a fairly sheltered position, where it will happily spread.

Dianthus

There are many delightful alpine pinks, all forming low mats or mounds with narrow leaves of green, grey or silver. Tiny ones for troughs, reaching 5 × 10cm (2 × 4in), include D. 'Berlin Snow' with short stems of fringed white flowers over a tight mat of thin green leaves and D. 'Nyewood's Cream' with semi-prostrate stems of small, cream flowers. D. petraeus subsp. noeanus is a spiky cushion of linear leaves with slender stems of highly scented, fringed, white flowers.

Those growing to 7–10cm (3–4in) × 10–15cm (4–6in) include D. alpinus, with narrow, green leaves and large solitary flowers of rose crimson. 'Joan's Blood' is a stunning form, with flat mats of bronze-tinged foliage and deep red flowers with a black centre. D. callizonus is a beautiful choice species, having large lavender-pink flowers attractively marked purple with white flecks, borne on short stems over light green tufts. It requires very gritty soil to grow well. Other small pinks are 'La Bourboule' (pink); 'Dainty Dame' (white, cherry-red centre); 'Whatfield Magenta' (bright magenta flowers, silver foliage); 'Whatfield Wisp' (faint pink blush, fringed petals); and 'Whatfield Joy' (vivid pink, red eye, sweetly scented).

Slightly larger pinks, up to 15 × 20–30cm (6 × 8–12in), can be grown in well-drained borders as well as raised beds, gravel and containers. D. 'Dewdrop' has sweetly scented, fringed, white flowers with a green eye over blue-grey foliage. D. deltoides and its many named forms have mats of green leaves with numerous small flowers, and will seed freely. 'Albus' (white) and 'Brilliant' (carmine) are just two examples.

Dianthus 'Whatfield Joy'

Diascia

Attractive alpines with spurred flowers, though usually not winter-hardy. In light, well-drained soil and a sheltered, sunny spot, the following may survive. D. integerrima (30 × 30cm; 12 × 12in) has deep salmon-pink flowers on slender upright stems of narrow leaves. D. lilacina (23 × 30cm; 9 × 12in) forms a low mound of hairy, slightly sticky, rounded leaves and has masses of dainty, lilac flowers. D. barberae 'Ruby Field' (15–20 × 25cm; 6–8 × 10in) is very floriferous, bearing dark salmon-pink flowers over dark green foliage, and is excellent for trailing, but is not reliably hardy. D. 'Lilac Belle' (15 × 30cm; 6 × 12in or more) forms a spreading mat with a long succession of small lilac flowers, and seems to be quite hardy. Take cuttings of diascias in late summer for overwintering in frost-free conditions.

Dodecatheon

Known as Shooting Stars, these have rosettes of
long, fleshy leaves and tall stems of drooping
flowers with swept-back petals. They thrive in a
moist, shady spot, but will grow in sun as long as
the soil does not dry out. They die back in winter,
and can be raised from seed. *D. meadia* has
25–45cm (10–18in) stems of rose-purple flowers,
and there is also a white form. *D. dentatum* (23cm;
9in) has pale green leaves and white flowers, while
D. pulchellum (20–25cm; 8–10in) is robust and free-
flowering, with flowers in shades of rose or red.

Dryas

The well-known Mountain Avens, *D. octopetala*
(8 × 30cm; 3½ × 12in or more), is a creeping,
woody, evergreen carpet of dark green, glossy, oak-
like leaves that are whitish beneath. It bears large,
wide open, white flowers with prominent yellow
stamens, followed by feathery seed-heads, and is an
easy, reliable plant for a sunny spot where it has
plenty of room to spread. *D. octopetala* 'Minor' is a
compact form (3 × 10–15cm; 1 × 4–6in), smaller
in all its parts, and can be grown in a trough.

Draba

Cushion alpines with a huge number of species,
often grown in the alpine house, but there are
several you can grow in the open in a well-drained
trough or raised bed. Any with woolly foliage
should be protected from winter wet. They can be
grown from seed, and you will find more unusual
species in specialist nurseries and at alpine shows.
D. aizoides (5 × 15cm; 2 × 6in) is an easy beginner's
plant, with bright lemon-yellow flowers over tufts
of deep green, rigid, narrow leaves. *D. rigida* var.
bryoides (4 × 6cm; 1½ × 2½in) has golden flowers
and dense cushions of tiny leaves.

Epilobium crassum

A tiny willowherb with glossy, red-edged leaves and
pink flowers followed by silky seeds. More or less
prostrate, it grows into a neat mat up to 10cm
(4in) across and readily seeds itself. It thrives in
raised beds or peat beds, in a position out of the
heat of the midday sun.

Erigeron

Erinus alpinus

E. alpinus forms a basal cluster of long, hairy leaves, spreading to 20cm (8in), with 15–20cm (6–8in) stems of pinkish-mauve rayed flowers with a yellow centre. *E. compositus* var. *discoideus* (7 × 7cm; 3 × 3in) is a lovely dwarf species for raised beds or troughs, with tufts of lobed, segmented, woolly leaves and pale lavender-blue flowers freely borne from late spring onwards, followed by fluffy seed-heads. It readily self-seeds, forming small colonies, giving a long season of soft colour. *E. acer debilis* (5 × 10cm; 2 × 4in) is a more unusual plant, with tufts of long, narrow leaves and masses of little pinkish-white flowers. *E.* 'Four Winds' (15 × 25cm; 6 × 10in) is a robust form with light pinky-mauve blooms over mats of dense foliage, and is suitable for the front of borders or gravel areas. It can be increased by division.

The Fairy Foxglove is a dainty plant with tufts of divided leaves, 5–7cm (2–3in) high with a similar spread, and many little, rosy-purple flowers. It is perennial, but sometimes short-lived, although it seeds around readily, so you are unlikely to lose it. There are various forms, such as var. *albus* (white), 'Dr Hahnle' (bright carmine) and 'Mrs Charles Boyle' (pure pink). They are very pretty for growing in gravel, raised beds and cracks in paving or walls.

Erigeron compositus **var.** *discoideus*

Erodium

Long-flowering, mounded alpines closely related to *Geranium*, these are attractive, relatively easygoing additions to raised beds, troughs, gravel areas and walls. Some form low cushions (3–7 × 10–20cm; 1–3 × 4–8in) of small, oak-like, dark green leaves almost continually smothered in rounded flowers veined with pinkish-purple. *E. reichardii* is white, *E. × variabile* 'Bishop's Form' has very bright, deep rose-pink flowers, and there is a tiny double pink form 'Flore Pleno'. Other species form more substantial mounds. *E. guttatum* (15 × 20cm; 6 × 8in) has velvety, grey-green, toothed leaves and long stems carrying white flowers, the upper two petals blotched deep maroon. *E. chrysanthum* (15 × 20cm; 6 × 8in) forms mounds of finely divided, silvery-green leaves, with soft sulphur-yellow flowers. It does not always flower freely, but makes an extremely attractive foliage plant anyway. Species can be raised from seed, named forms from semi-ripe cuttings.

Frankenia thymifolia

Forming a prostrate mat up to 20cm (8in) or so of tiny, grey-green leaves, this is ideal for the edge of a trough or raised bed, or a carpet on gravel areas. Clusters of tiny, rose-pink, stemless flowers appear in summer, and the foliage becomes distinctly red-tinted during autumn.

Erodium × variabile **'Bishop's Form'**

Gentiana

A large genus, containing spring-flowering species for sun and well-drained soil, and autumn-flowering Asiatic gentians for moist, peaty soil in partial shade. *G. verna* is the lovely spring gentian, though it can be difficult to grow in cultivation, forming loose tufts with starry deep blue flowers on 5–8cm (2–3in) stems. It needs light, gritty soil and resents disturbance. *G. acaulis*, the trumpet gentian, is well known as the symbol of the Alpine Garden Society in the UK, and grows as low mats (8 × 10cm; 3 × 4in or more) of evergreen leaves, bearing solitary, large funnel-shaped flowers of deep blue, marked greenish-brown inside. It prefers heavy but well-drained soil in full sun and should be firmly planted. It often fails to flower, and needs moving around until you find somewhere it can thrive. *G. saxosa* (7 × 15cm; 3 × 6in) is a New Zealand species, with white flowers in late summer over glossy, dark green, bronzed leaves, and is lovely in a sunny trough. It requires light soil that does not dry out. *G. septemfida* (15 × 30cm; 6 × 12in) is one of the easiest species, tolerating most soils, even heavy clay. It has leafy, spreading stems and heads of flowers in varying shades of blue borne in late summer. *G. sino-ornata* (5–10cm; 2–4in) has rosettes of narrow, pointed leaves and long, prostrate stems, each carrying an upright, trumpet-shaped flower of rich blue. It requires rich, lime-free, moisture-retentive soil, where it will form wide mats 30cm (12in) or more across covered in flowers from early autumn. There are numerous cultivars to choose from, including 'Angel's Wings' (large bright blue striped white), 'Alba' and 'Mary Lyle' (white) and 'Edith Sarah' (rich blue feathered white). *G. ternifolia* (5 × 30cm; 2 × 12in) is a beautiful, floriferous Chinese species, with blue trumpets which are striped green and white outside. 'Cangshan' and 'Dali' are two available cultivars, both requiring similar conditions to *G. sino-ornata*. Divide the autumn-flowering gentians every three years in spring. Propagate others by division or seed.

Gentiana acaulis

Geranium

☀ ● |◔◔| | | 🏵🏵🏵🏵🏵🏵🏵 | | |

There are many small geraniums suitable for
alpine plantings, although some do need room to
spread, being ideal at the front of a border or in a
gravel area. Their mounds of dense foliage are
studded with flowers for long periods, often well
into autumn. *G. sanguineum* var. *striatum*
(15 × 30cm; 6 × 12in) has masses of clear pink
flowers over neat, dark foliage and thrives in sun
or shade, forming an excellent edging or ground
cover under the base of shrubs. There is a white
form, 'Album', while 'Max Frei' has deep magenta
flowers – both are slightly taller at 20cm (8in).
G. dalmaticum is small enough for troughs, growing
to 10 × 15cm (4 × 6in), and has glossy green
leaves that take on rich autumn tints, and pretty
pink flowers. There is also an attractive white
form. *G. cinereum* (15 × 30cm; 6 × 12in) has grey-
green leaves and pale, lilac-pink blooms veined in
deeper pink. There are several popular cultivars
and hybrids, including 'Ballerina' (lilac flowers
with deep purple centres over silvery green
mounds), 'Laurence Flatman' (pink, heavily striped
purple), and subsp. *subcaulescens* var. *subcaulescens*
(brilliant cerise, dark centres). *G. sessiliflorum* subsp.
novae-zelandiae 'Nigricans' (7 × 15cm; 3 × 6in)
forms dense mats of chocolate-brown leaves, some
turning orange in winter, with small white flowers
nestling among them. It makes good foliage
contrast, but does seed itself freely.

Geranium cinereum **subsp.** *subcaulescens* **var.** *subcaulescens*

Geranium cinereum **'Laurence Flatman'**

Geranium dalmaticum

Geum

☀ ☼ ◖◖

There are a couple of species suitable for raised beds or peat beds, with pinnate leaves and cup-shaped flowers. *G. montanum*, the alpine avens, has soft, green leaves with a large terminal leaflet, and rich, golden yellow flowers 3cm (1in) across, and grows to 12 × 30cm (5 × 12in). An unusual little species is *G. pentapetalum* (7 × 23cm; 3 × 9in), with green leaves that take on orange-gold tones during autumn, and creamy white flowers.

Gypsophila

☀ ◖

Trailing gypsophilas are invaluable for raised beds, walls and containers, while the dwarf cushion types add interest with their neat leaves and rounded flowers. *G. repens* (7 × 20–30cm; 3 × 8–12in) has prostrate stems clothed in neat blue-green or grey-green leaves, and carries many sprays of little flowers. 'Dubia' and 'Rosea' are soft pink, the former having attractive red-tinged stems, and there is a white-flowered form. 'Fratensis' is a neater, less vigorous form with pink flowers, ideal for the edge of a trough. *G. cerastioides* (5 × 15cm; 2 × 6in) has pretty, white purple-veined flowers above dense, low mats of velvety, green foliage. *G. aretioides* forms hard cushions of tiny leaves, but usually does not flower freely, while 'Caucasica' forms even tighter, harder domes. Both require well-drained soil in full sun to succeed outside.

Helianthemum

☀ ◖

Rock roses have a range of bright or pastel flowers, providing splashes of colour for long periods. They are evergreen, shrubby plants with green or grey, narrow leaves, relishing hot, dry positions and thriving even in poor soils. They grow to 15–20 × 15–20cm (6–8 × 6–8in). Recommended named forms include 'Ben Ledi' (deep rose-red), 'Ben Fhada' (yellow, orange centre), 'Sudbury Gem' (deep pink), 'The Bride' (white), 'Sterntaler' (large golden-yellow) and 'Wisley Primrose' (soft yellow). Prune hard after flowering to prevent legginess. *H. lunulatum* is a much smaller, neater species (7 × 15cm; 3 × 6in) with prostrate stems of greyish leaves and many small, showy yellow flowers. *H. oelandicum* subsp. *alpestre* is even tinier, and both these can be grown in troughs.

Gypsophila repens **white**

114

Helichrysum bellidiodes

☀ ⊔ | | | | ▦▦ | | | | |

With its papery 'everlasting' flowers and hairy leaves, this is well adapted to its native habitat of hot, arid conditions. The prostrate stems are clothed in silvery, woolly leaves, with creamy flowers, and will spread widely in a hot, sunny position, reaching 23cm (9in) or more across.

Hypsela reniformis

● ⍟ | | ▦▦ | | | | | |

A carpeting plant with bright green, kidney-shaped, fleshy leaves, 2 × 20cm (1 × 8in), rooting down as it spreads. It bears small lobed flowers of pink with crimson markings, and prefers shade and moist, peaty soil in a fairly sheltered spot. 'Greencourt White' is a white-flowered form.

Hypericum

☀ ◖◗ | | | ▦▦▦ | | | | |

There are several small alpine forms, bearing characteristic yellow flowers with a central mass of prominent stamens. They vary from upright shrubby bushes to prostrate mats. *H. olympicum* (20 × 15cm; 8 × 6in) is an easy, reliable, bushy form with glaucous leaves and large golden-yellow flowers borne over many weeks in summer. *H. olympicum* f. *minus* 'Sulphureum' (15cm; 6in) is similar, with beautiful soft lemon-yellow flowers. *H. reptans* (3 × up to 20cm; 1 × 8in) produces slender, prostrate stems of bronze, red-tinged leaves, ending in round, rich golden flowers opening from red buds. This can grow as a flat mat, or will hang as a leafy sheet down the sides of a trough or raised bed. *H. empetrifolium* subsp. *tortuosum* is a low, creeping form 2 × 15cm (½ × 6in) with densely packed stems of tiny leaves and rich golden flowers. *H. cerastioides* is a neat species for a trough, forming 15–20cm (6–8in) wide mats of hairy foliage covered in bright yellow flowers on 5cm (2in) stems.

Hypericum cerastioides

Iberis

Iberis aurosiaca **'Sweetheart'**

The perennial alpine candytufts are easy, floriferous plants for well-drained border edges, raised beds and walls. They grow as somewhat woody subshrubs, with leathery, evergreen leaves, the stems often spreading into wide mats. The flattened flower heads are composed of many small white or pinkish flowers. *I. sempervirens* (15–30 × 30–45cm; 6–12 × 12–18in or more) has narrow, thick leaves with pure white flowers, and there are several named cultivars, including 'Schneeflocke' and 'Weisser Zwerg', the latter more compact with deep green foliage. *I. aurosiaca* 'Sweetheart' is a compact, dark green cushion smothered in pink flowers, turning lilac, and reaches 10 × 15cm (4 × 6in). Grow from seed or semi-ripe cuttings and cut back quite hard after flowering.

Ionopsidium acaule

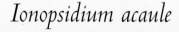

A very pretty annual alpine, worth growing for its mass of dainty little lilac flowers borne over a long period. It is easy to raise from seed, ideally sowing straight into the soil, either in cracks in paving, or in patches on a raised bed or gravel area. It forms tiny tufts of spoon-shaped leaves, only 5cm (2in) high.

Ionopsidium acaule

116

Jasione

With tufts spreading to 10–20cm (4–8in), *J. laevis* is a robust plant with mostly basal leaves, narrow and roughly hairy, and 20–30cm (8–12in) stems with fewer, smaller leaves rising up to carry the globose, bright blue flower heads, which are attractive to butterflies. 'Blaulicht' is an especially fine form with deep blue flowers. *J. heldreichii* has smaller leaves and clear blue flowers on 20cm (8in) stems. Easy from seed, or increase by division.

Leontopodium

L. alpinum is the well-known Edelweiss, growing to 10–20cm (4–8in) tall by 15cm (6in), with tufts of narrow, grey-green leaves. The distinctive flower heads are made up of small yellowish-white flowers in the centre, surrounded by whitish-grey, woolly, leafy bracts. 'Mignon' is a neater form with low carpets of leaves and short stems of 10cm (4in). They dislike wet soils at any time and can be short-lived. Propagate by seed, which can produce variable plants, or by division.

Jovibarba

Closely related to *Sempervivum*, these form clusters of small, symmetrical rosettes, about 3cm (1in) in height, with tiny, fleshy, incurving leaves and 10cm (4in) stems of bell-shaped flowers on mature plants. *J. sobolifera*, known as the hen-and-chickens houseleek, has small, green rosettes with red-tipped leaves, yellow flowers and numerous offsets clustering all around, detaching easily and rooting where they fall. *J. arenaria* is one of the smallest species, with tiny, green rosettes. *J. hirta* var. *glabrescens* has semi-open rosettes of sharply pointed yellow-green leaves, and bold heads of bright yellow flowers.

Leptinella

Creeping ground cover with ferny leaves and little, inconspicuous, yellow pinhead flowers. *L. potentillina* has deeply divided green and bronze leaves, while *L. squalida* is more olive green in colour. Both form completely flat carpets, rooting as they spread, and can be useful in cracks in paving or in shady corners, though they can be invasive in a restricted area.

Lewisia

These showy alpines will thrive outside given the right conditions of well-drained, humus-rich, gritty soil in a cool position. They have basal rosettes of fleshy leaves, which may rot during a wet winter, so they are best grown on a slope to allow excess water to drain away easily (e.g. the side of a wall, a raised bed or between rocks) or covered with a sheet of glass in winter. *L. cotyledon* has broad evergreen leaves, and 10–15cm (4–6in) stems of many rounded flowers in a range of colours: pinks, yellows, orange, white, magenta. Many ranges, such as Sunset Group and Ashwood strain, have been bred. Some are solid colours, while others may be striped, or have notched petals or semi-double flowers. *L. cantelovii* has small rosettes of distinctive sharply toothed leaves, and sprays of many small pale pink flowers striped deeper pink. *L columbiana* has rosettes of narrow, smooth leaves and thin 25–30cm (10–12in) stems of small, delicately pink-striped white flowers, produced in profusion. Two deciduous species worth trying, both with narrow, linear leaves that die back after flowering, are *L. nevadensis* with large white flowers at soil level in early summer, and *L. pygmaea*, which has short stems of striped magenta flowers. There are also many showy hybrids, including 'George Henley' (rich rose-purple). Most species grow readily from seed, though they hybridize easily, so if you grow several together you will probably raise some interesting variations. Named forms need to be propagated by rooting offsets.

Lewisia cotyledon

Limonium

There are several dwarf statice, easily raised from seed, with leathery, spatula-shaped leaves in basal rosettes, and sprays of papery flowers on slender, branching, wiry stems. *L. bellidifolium* has rounded rosettes and pinkish-mauve flowers on 10–20cm (4–8in) stems. *L. minutum* forms tiny cushions of dark green leaves, with 5–10cm (2–4in) wiry stems of fine, papery, pale violet-blue flowers, an excellent miniature for troughs. Other species to look for are *L. cosyrense* and *L. gougetianum*, both with pinkish blooms. All are good later flowering alpines for raised beds or troughs.

Linum

☀ ◔ | | | ▦ ▦ ▦ | | | | | |

The flaxes are slender, tufted plants ideal for well-drained, sunny sites. *L. perenne* 'Blau Saphir' is a dwarf form of the species, with 20–30cm (8–12in) stems of grey-green foliage and clear blue, saucer-shaped flowers. 'Diamant' is a similar pure white cultivar, and both can be raised from seed. Both are excellent planted in groups on gravel areas, where they will self-seed. *L.* 'Gemmell's Hybrid' is a choice, compact plant (15 × 20cm; 6 × 8in) with a hummock of blue-green foliage and many clusters of bright, deep golden flowers.

Linum perenne **'Blau Saphir'**

Lithodora

☀ ◔ | | ▦ ▦ | | | | | | |

Previously known as *Lithospermum*, these shrubby evergreens have funnel-shaped, usually blue flowers, produced in the leaf axils. *L. diffusa* is a prostrate mat 10–20 × up to 60cm (4–8 × 24in), clothed in slender, dark green, bristly leaves, usually available as named forms, including 'Heavenly Blue' (large, deep blue flowers), 'Grace Ward' (even richer blue) and 'Alba' (white). These require an acid or neutral soil in a sunny, sheltered spot, where they will provide sheets of colour during early summer. *L. oleifolia* (20cm; 8in) has silky, grey-green leaves and pink buds opening to sky-blue flowers, and will grow on limy soil. All can be propagated by semi-ripe cuttings after flowering.

Mentha requienii

◑ ● ◖◗◗ | | ▦ ▦ | | | | | |

The tiny Spanish or Corsican mint (1 × 20cm or more; ½ × 8in), forming fresh green carpets of rounded leaves, strongly peppermint-scented, and studded with microscopic stemless lavender flowers. An excellent plant for crevices and paving, or gravel areas in moist shade.

Minuartia

Cushion alpines ideal for raised beds and troughs. *M. circassica* (10 × 15cm; 4 × 6in) has very fine grassy leaves with loose clusters of white flowers. *M. stellata* has dense, bright green foliage packed to form tight, hard cushions (2 × 15cm; 1 × 6in), and bears almost stemless white flowers. It makes an interesting addition to a trough.

Mitella

These little plants are ideal for shady spots in damp soil, forming low mounds of long-stalked leaves and carrying stems of white, greenish or yellowish flowers with fringed petals. *M. breweri* has dark green lobed leaves covered in short hairs, and numerous 15–20cm (6–8in) long sprays of little greenish flowers. *M. diphylla* (23cm; 9in) has glossy, lobed leaves and spikes of white flowers. *M. caulescens* (10–15cm; 4–6in) bears toothed, heart-shaped leaves and drooping pale yellow flowers. Raise from seed or increase by division.

Mitella breweri

Minuartia circassica

Origanum

There are several small shrubby origanums for alpine gardens, with heads of tiny flowers in conspicuous bracts, often very attractive in themselves. *O. microphyllum* (10–12 × 15cm; 4–5 × 6in) is clothed in small, silvery, aromatic leaves and has many wiry stems carrying spikelets of pinkish-mauve flowers in grey bracts. It is neat enough for a trough, where its late flowering is valuable. *O.* 'Buckland' has an upright habit, with softly hairy green leaves and long slender pink flowers surrounded by dainty pink-tinged bracts. Growing to 23 × 20cm (9 × 8in) or so, it has proved hardy in a sunny trough of gritty soil. *O. rotundifolium* (7–10 × 30cm; 3–4 × 12in) has smooth, rounded, blue-green leaves clasping short stems, and drooping heads of pale pink tubular flowers encased in conspicuous pale apple-green bracts, which remain attractive for a long period.

Oxalis

Decorative trefoil leaves are an attraction of many species of this genus, though they vary widely and any invasive types should be avoided. *O. magellanica* has tiny, bronzed green shamrock leaves and relatively large pure white stemless flowers, and its prostrate, creeping habit makes it ideal for paving cracks in a cool position. There is also a pretty double-flowered form. *O. adenophylla* grows from fibre-coated tubers, producing intricately pleated blue-grey leaves, followed by wide, goblet-shaped flowers of satiny lilac-pink veined deeper pink. Only 5–7 × 10cm (2–3 × 4in), it thrives in full sun in a rich soil, benefiting from a top dressing in spring as the tuber tends to work its way to the surface. *O. enneaphylla* (5 × 10cm; 2 × 4in) has crinkled silver-grey leaves and large white flowers, while 'Rosea' has beautiful rose-pink flowers. These are wonderful in raised beds or troughs.

Oxalis adenophylla

Papaver

There are a few small poppies suitable for alpine plantings, though they tend to be short-lived perennials, usually self-seeding freely. Wonderful in patches in hot, gravel gardens or among cracks in paving. The alpine poppy, *P. alpinum*, is variable, with tufts of glaucous, finely cut leaves and 10cm (4in) stems of dainty flowers of white, yellow, orange or pink. *P. miyabeanum* 'Pacino' is easily raised from seed, having large soft yellow flowers on 15cm (6in) stems above hairy, light green foliage. It is long-flowering, and grows well in raised beds, troughs or gravel. *P. rupifragum* is a taller species from Spain, with soft orange flowers on 15–30cm (6–12in) stems, and tufts of light grey-green leaves.

Origanum **'Buckland'**

Parahebe

Reliable, long-flowering evergreen bushes up to 15cm (6in) high by 20–30cm (8–12in) wide, clothed in leathery, toothed foliage and bearing sprays of delicate flowers, veined crimson or pink, for much of the year. *P. catarractae* 'Delight' is lilac-blue, and there is also a white form; 'Rosea' is lower growing with pink flowers. *P. lyallii* is low and spreading, with mounds of thick, leathery, dark green leaves and masses of white, pink-veined flowers; *P. lyallii* 'Julie-Anne' is more compact, with small, neat, toothed leaves of bright green, and is free-flowering with masses of dainty white flowers. All are excellent plants for raised beds, front of border, containers or gravel gardens. Propagate by cuttings.

Parahebe lyallii

Penstemon

A large genus of semi-shrubby or herbaceous plants with lipped flowers like snapdragons. The smaller types are excellent for alpine gardens, their showy flowers borne over a long period. *P. newberryi* is a low mat (10–15 × up to 30cm; 4–6 × 12in) with downy young stems and leathery, green leaves, bearing bright cerise-crimson funnel-shaped flowers in mid-summer. *P. fruticosus* var. *scouleri* (up to 30cm; 12in in height and width) is upright growing with narrow leaves and many lavender flowers during early summer, and there is a white-flowered form. Two reliable pink-flowered hybrids are 'Six Hills' and 'Pink Dragon' (both 20–30cm; 8–12in). *P. pinifolius* is very distinctive, forming a low bush 10–20cm (4–8in) in height by 15cm (6in), of needle-like foliage with narrow, tubular, scarlet flowers. 'Mersea Yellow' is a lovely form, bearing bright yellow tubular flowers, and 'Wisley Flame' is slightly larger (20–25cm; 8–10in) with longer leaves and bright orange-red tubular flowers.

Persicaria vaccinifolia

Excellent for colour and interest late in the season, and useful for ground cover or trailing over walls, this forms a twiggy mat of small leaves bearing numerous spikes of bright rose-pink flowers over a long period. The leaves turn red and bronze before falling in autumn. It grows to 23cm (9in) high with a much wider spread.

Phlox

The many cultivars of *P. douglasii* form compact
tufted cushions (5 × 15cm; 2 × 6in) of needle-like
green leaves, hidden in late spring under a mass of
colourful flowers. They are found in a wide range
of colours: 'Red Admiral' and 'Crackerjack' are
brilliant crimson-red, 'Iceberg' is pale ice blue,
'Rosea' is pale pink and 'Violet Queen' is rich violet.
All are excellent for troughs, planted at the edges to
tumble over. *P. kelseyi* 'Rosette' is a pretty form of a
similar size for a trough or raised bed, with narrow
foliage in a compact mat and rounded pink flowers.
P. subulata (7–10 × 15–20cm; 3–4 × 6–8in) forms
more spreading, leafy mats, covered in larger
flowers, available in many colours. 'Amazing Grace'
has lovely white flowers flushed pink, with a darker
eye; 'Temiskaming' is rosy red and 'McDaniel's
Cushion' has fresh green foliage studded with large
pink flowers. *P.* × *procumbens* 'Variegata' (12cm; 5in)
has striking cream-variegated leaves and deep pink
flowers. Propagate by cuttings.

Phlox douglasii **'Crackerjack'**

Phyteuma

Typically having grassy or toothed, narrow leaves
with heads of narrow-petalled flowers, often curved
and bearing long bracts, these are more unusual
alpines to try. *P. scheuchzeri*, growing to 20–30cm
(8–12in), has 10cm (4in) wide tufts of blue-green
leaves, the basal ones heart-shaped and the upper
ones long and slender. It has stunning deep blue,
dense flower heads with long, pointed bracts below.
P. hemisphaericum (15cm; 6in) has dense tufts of grassy
leaves and dark, violet-blue flowers with short bracts.

Persicaria vaccinifolia

Phyteuma scheuchzeri

Potentilla

Easily grown, mostly low-growing alpines with lobed leaves, producing numerous flowers when planted in a sunny spot. There are several yellow-flowered species, often difficult to tell apart. *P. eriocarpa* (5 × 15cm; 2 × 6in) has clear yellow flowers on short stems above spreading mats of small, grey-green leaves, and is ideal for growing in crevices or as a small carpeting plant. *P. cuneata* (5 × 30cm; 2 × 12in) has wide spreading mats of foliage covered in golden flowers, useful for ground cover and front of border. *P. × tonguei* (10 × 25cm; 4 × 10in) has long, trailing stems with dark green leaves and attractive apricot flowers with a crimson centre, borne over many weeks. *P. nitida* has beautiful silvery leaves and relatively large rose-pink flowers, not always flowering freely but quite easy to grow on lime-enriched soil. It grows 3–5cm (1–2in) high, spreading 20cm (8in).

Pratia

Dense, creeping mats that root as they go, making propagation by division easy. They require moist soil that is well drained, thriving in partial shade at the foot of a wall or peat bed, or in cracks and crevices in paving or steps.

Plant them where they won't swamp neighbouring alpines, particularly *P. pedunculata*, which can grow into large mats. This has soft, light green foliage covered in masses of pale blue star-shaped flowers, very pretty over a long period. The form 'County Park' has blue-green foliage and rich, violet-blue, fragrant flowers. *P. angulata* has pale green, somewhat fleshy, leaves on pinkish stems and stemless white, lobelia-like flowers that are followed by bright purple berries. 'Treadwellii' is larger in all its parts. All are about 1cm (½ in) high with an indefinite spread.

Primula × pubescens **'Christine'**

Primula

There is a huge number of species in this genus, but here are some of the hardy, reliable ones to grow in the open garden. *P. auricula* is variable, but has some beautiful forms, so choose plants in flower. Rosettes of large, soft, grey-green leaves, sometimes covered in white 'bloom', carry 10–15cm (4–6in) stems of flowers. The type species has yellow flowers with a mealy eye; others include 'Old Yellow Dusty Miller' (yellow with white eye) and 'Paradise Yellow' (golden yellow). There are also several strains that contain a mixture of colours. *P. denticulata*, the drumstick primula, has large leaves in clumps spreading to 30cm (12in) or more and stout 10–25cm (4–10in) stems of mauve, purple or white flowers in a globular head, and is ideal for a peat bed or border. There are many named varieties of *P. × pubescens* (10 × 10–15cm; 4 × 4–6in), resembling miniature auriculas, suitable for troughs and raised beds in partial shade. 'Bewerley White' (creamy colour),

'Boothman's Variety' (bright crimson) and 'Faldonside' (reddish-pink, white eye) are among those readily available. *P. marginata* (10–15 × 10–20cm; 4–6 × 4-8in) has toothed leaves with silver margins, and loose heads of lavender or violet flowers, each with a white eye; 'Caerulea' is a form with blue flowers.

The Bird's-eye Primrose, *P. farinosa*, is a beautiful little species, 5–15cm (2–6in) tall by 15cm (6in), with small leaves, white underneath, and neat heads of lilac-pink yellow-eyed flowers. *P. frondosa* is larger (10–18cm; 4–7in), with crinkled leaf margins and loose heads of reddish-purple flowers, each with a yellow eye. Both are early flowering, preferring moisture-retentive soil, and grow well in a peat bed. The lovely *P. reidii* var. *williamsii* needs to be kept dry during winter, or its rosettes of soft, woolly leaves tend to rot, so cover it with a piece of glass or a small cloche. It has scented, nodding flowers of pale blue, held in tight heads on 10cm (4in) stems.

Pterocephalus perennis

Pterocephalus perennis

A beautiful, low, tufted plant with felted, grey-green, toothed leaves, that can form a mat or be allowed to trail down the side of a raised bed. Pale mauvy-pink scabious-like flowers are borne in profusion on very short stems, followed by feathery seed-heads. It grows only 7cm (3in) high, spreading to 20–30cm (8–12in), and is very long-flowering. Propagate by cuttings.

Pulsatilla

☼ |◊◊| | ❋ ❋ | | | | | | | |

The pasque flowers are best grown from seed or obtained as young plants, as they resent disturbance once established. The long taproot can easily be damaged, so choose a spot in full sun where the flowers can be appreciated in spring and don't move them once planted. *P. vulgaris* (20 × 20cm; 8 × 8in) has finely dissected leaves, with silky buds opening to rich purple, goblet-shaped flowers, each with a central golden mass of stamens, followed by feathery seed-heads on elongating stems. Forms include 'Eva Constance' (large red flowers) and 'Alba' (pure white). *P. vernalis* (10cm; 4in) has white flowers, flushed pink or violet outside and covered in woolly hairs. The buds appear in late winter, so may need protection from winter wet. You may find several exciting species offered as seed from specialist sources, all of which are worth trying. Seed may take time to germinate, so be patient.

Pulsatilla vulgaris **'Alba'**

Ranunculus gramineus

Ranunculus

☼ |◊| | | ❋ ❋ ❋ ❋ | | | | |

R. gramineus is distinctive, with its tufts of narrow foliage and slender 20–30cm (8–12in) stems of rich yellow buttercup flowers in summer. It is lovely in raised beds or gravel areas, where it will self-seed. *R. crenatus* (5 × 10cm; 2 × 4in) forms small, rounded tufts of heart-shaped leaves and bears quite large white flowers in late spring. It is ideal for troughs, requiring full sun and well-drained, gritty compost.

Saponaria × olivana

Raoulia

These Australasian alpines have minute rosettes of leaves in dense cushions, forming wide mats in the wild. In cultivation, they spread less freely and require overhead protection from excess winter wet. They have insignificant white or yellowish flowers. Grow in gritty soil in full sun, in a trough or raised bed or on tufa rock. Species to look for include *R. australis*, with silvery grey leaves; *R. hookeri*, with pale green, intensely silver leaves and *R. haastii*, with rich green rosettes in hard mounds, turning brown in winter.

Saponaria

Colourful, easily grown alpines for a wide range of situations. The leafy trailing 20cm (8in) stems of 'Tumbling Ted', *Saponaria ocymoides*, form a carpet or a cascading mat, and are covered in bright pink flowers giving a wonderful display of colour. There is a white form 'Snow Tip', equally floriferous, and both are good trailing plants for raised beds or containers. *S. × olivana* has bright green cushions of foliage covered in short-stemmed, large, pale pink flowers, making an attractive mound of 5 × 10cm (2 × 4in) for a smaller space. *S.* 'Rosenteppich' (5 × 10cm; 2 × 4in) has masses of large, deep pink flowers covering a compact mat of leafy prostrate stems.

Saxifraga

Early flowering saxifrages have tight rosettes of leaves and flowers in many colours, often very early in the year, and are 5–7cm (2–3in) high and about 10cm (4in) across. There are numerous ones available, of which just a few are mentioned here. *S. × anglica* 'Myra' is blue-grey with stemless deep pink flowers, *S. × irvingii* 'Jenkinsiae' has tight silver-grey hummocks with large, shell-pink flowers and *S. × webriii* 'Pygmalion' has light yellow flowers above bright green, lime-encrusted rosettes. *S. × salmonica* 'Mrs Helen Terry' has white flowers over cushions of silvery green, needle-like leaves and *S. burseriana* 'Prince Hal' has large white blooms on salmon-pink stems. *S. × hardingii* 'Iris Prichard' is a distinctive very early flowering one with silver encrusted rosettes and buff-apricot flowers.

The silver saxifrages have encrusted rosettes, often with spoon-shaped leaves, their mounds spreading to 20cm (8in) or so, and carry many sprays of dainty flowers in late spring and early summer. *S. × burnatii* 'Esther' has creamy yellow flowers on 15cm (6in) horizontal stems and 'Doctor Ramsey' has handsome silvered rosettes with white flowers on 20cm (8in) stems. *S. cochlearis* 'Minor' has minute, silver rosettes in tight, hard cushions with white flowers on 10cm (4in) stems. *S.* 'Whitehill' is a reliable, attractive form with silvery grey-blue rosettes, flushed red at the base, bearing dense, white flowers on reddish stems of 15–20cm (6–8in).

Other types include 'Winifred Bevington' (15cm; 6in) with tidy green rosettes and sprays of white pink-spotted flowers in summer. The larger London Pride, *S. × urbium* (25cm; 10in high, with a wider spread), bears masses of dainty, starry white flowers spotted red over dense rosettes, and looks well in peat beds, borders or as path edging. 'Clarence Elliott' is smaller (15cm; 6in) with rose-pink flowers. All these are suitable for partially shaded spots in raised beds, sinks and pans.

The mossy saxifrages have rosettes of notched leaves, forming dense mats or cushions 10–30cm (4–12in) or more across, flowering in spring, and grow in sun or partial shade in soil that does not dry out. Old mats tend to brown in the centre, so replant the outer, fresher growth every 2–3 years and discard the centre. There are numerous hybrids, widely available, creating splashes of colour in spring. These include 'Carnival' (red, 20cm; 8in), 'Gaiety' (pink, 10cm; 4in) and 'Pearly King' (clear white, 10cm; 4in). *S. exarata* subsp. *moschata* 'Cloth of Gold' is compact with golden foliage and white flowers (10cm; 4in), best grown in some shade to prevent scorching.

Propagate saxifrages by rooting individual rosettes in sharp, gritty compost, making sure to keep them shaded.

Scabiosa

☀ 🌢🌢 | | | | | ✽✽✽✽ | | |

There are some lovely small scabious for alpine gardens, valuable for their succession of flowers over a long period. They self-seed freely, so remove the rounded honeycomb seed heads if you want to control their spread. The flowers are particularly attractive to bees and butterflies, and as they are mostly soft shades of mauve and lavender, they will blend into most schemes. *S. japonica* var. *alpina* (10–15cm; 4–6in) is a low tuft of toothed leaves bearing many lavender-blue flower heads. *S. graminifolia* is taller, up to 15–25cm (6–10in), with long, narrow silky-haired leaves and stiff stems of spherical lilac flower heads.

Scabiosa japonica **var.** *alpina*

Saxifraga × *irvingii* **'Jenkinsiae'**

Scleranthus biflorus

☀ ⌴ | | | | ✽✽✽ | | |

This dense, compact cushion plant has minute, green, needle-like leaves and tiny flowers in pairs, and will mound itself over rocks and even form irregular hummocks within itself. It is ideal for a large trough, raised bed or growing in a wide low pan, spreading 20–30cm (8–12in), but only 1cm (less than ½in) high. *S. uniflorus* is very similar, with solitary flowers. Both can be raised from seed.

Scutellaria pontica

Scutellaria

Easily grown alpines that are especially useful for their late, colourful flowers. They are spreading, tufted plants, with small, often toothed leaves and hooded, tubular flowers giving them their common name of skullcap. *S. alpina* (15–20 × 20cm; 6–8 × 8in) has deep purple flowers with a white lower lip, although some forms are paler in colour. Strains are also available with flowers of rose-pink, yellow and violet-blue. *S. orientalis* (10 × up to 30cm; 4 × up to 12in) has creeping stems of dark green leaves and dense clusters of long, bright yellow flowers, marked reddish-brown on the lower lip. The form subsp. *pinnatifida* is lovely, with delicate, greyish green foliage and yellow flowers. *S. prostrata* (5 × 20cm; 2 × 8in) forms a mat of tiny, serrated grey-green leaves, covered in many lavender and cream flowers, and is neat enough to grow over the edge of a trough. *S. scordiifolia* has stunning deep blue flowers above 15–20cm (6–8in) tufts, and *S. pontica* makes a low mat (5–7 × 15cm; 2–3 × 6in) of deep green foliage with many showy reddish-purple flowers. All are easily raised from seed.

Sedum

A huge genus, containing many alpine species with thick fleshy leaves and large heads of many starry flowers in late summer. *S. kamtschaticum* var. *floriferum* 'Weihenstephaner Gold' has dark green leafy stems carrying heads of golden starry flowers, turning reddish with age. *S. spurium* var. *album* has pale green foliage and pure white heads. *S. spurium* 'Variegatum' carries pale pink flowers and has colourful pink, cream and grey leaves, while 'Purpurteppich' has plum-purple leaves and deep pink flowers. All these are 5cm (2in) in height by 20–30cm (8–12in) in spread. *S.* 'Ruby Glow' has long, lax, radiating 25cm (10in) stems of green, purple-tinged succulent leaves, ending in deep rose-pink flowers. A neat form for a trough is *S. spathulifolium* 'Cape Blanco' with rosettes of rounded leaves covered in a thick white bloom and heads of yellow flowers on 5cm (2in) stems. The more unusual *S.* 'Silver Moon' is similar, but with larger rosettes. *S. oreganum* (5cm; 2in) forms a mound 15–20cm (6–8in) or more across of fat, glossy, globular leaves that turn bright red in full sun, and produces yellow flowers. Deciduous forms, dying back to resting buds over winter, with new growth arising from the base of old stems, include *S. kamtschaticum* var. *ellacombeanum* (5 × 20cm; 2 × 8in), with broad foliage of bright yellow-green and large heads of yellow flowers. Sedums root very easily from cuttings.

Sedum kamtschaticum **var.** *ellacombeanum*

Sedum oreganum

Sedum '**Silver Moon**'

Sempervivum

These succulent alpines have neat rosettes of leaves showing a wide range of subtle and bright colours, including deep red, soft mauve, olive and lime green. The leaves are sometimes tipped dark red or may change colour during the year, the richest and deepest colours usually showing in summer. Others have fine cobwebbing on the rosettes. Size varies from 3–15cm (1–6in) in height with a spread of 10–30cm (4–12in) or so, depending on type. Rosette size varies considerably, from tiny tight ones to large imposing forms. Reddish-brown, rose or yellow flowers are borne in summer, and although the main flowering rosette dies, numerous offsets are produced. There are thousands of named forms to choose from, and they all thrive in well-drained gritty soil in full sun. They are ideal for troughs, pans, raised beds and gravel areas. *S. arachnoideum* is the well-known cobweb houseleek, with tightly packed green and pink rosettes covered in white hairs and var. *bryoides* has tiny moss-like rosettes. *S. kosaninii* has flat, downy rosettes, the dark green leaves tipped purple, with offsets on long stolons. *S. tectorum* has many named forms, including 'Nigrum' with apple-green leaves heavily tipped reddish-purple, and 'Royanum' with large, yellowish-green rosettes. *S. calcareum* forms neat clusters of tidy rosettes: 'Limelight' has yellowish-green leaves tipped red, and 'Mrs Giuseppi' is grey-green with deep red tips. 'Grigg's Surprise' (formerly 'Monstrosum') is an unusual form with congested rosettes of fat, globular leaves, pale green with red tips.

The following suggestions give you some idea of the vast range of form and colour in named cultivars. 'Black Knight' has very deep dark red rosettes, appearing almost black; 'Blue Boy' is a muted grey-purple; 'Commander Hay' has large rosettes richly coloured red and green; 'Corsair' is flushed dark red; 'Red Devil' is a dark, glowing red; and 'Video' has flattish rosettes of grey-green, flushed purplish.

Individual rosettes can be rooted, though often you can detach side rosettes already rooted.

Sempervivum **'King George'**

Sempervivum **'Red Devil'**

Silene

Silene acaulis (2 × 15cm; 1 × 6in) is a cushion alpine, forming a mat of bright green thin leaves with small pink flowers on very short stems. An even smaller form is 'Mount Snowdon', a very tight cushion with minute pink flowers. *S. alpestris* (15 × 20cm; 6 × 8in) has neat tufts of foliage and branching sprays of dainty, white flowers with fringed petals; there is an equally attractive double form, 'Flore Pleno', with tightly double, white flowers and more rounded leaves. Propagate by seed or cuttings.

Sisyrinchium idahoense

Sisyrinchium

These have iris-like leaves in clumps spreading to 10cm (4in) or so and starry flowers in clusters that open in the sun. *S. idahoense* is a neat little species 10cm (4in) in height, with compact tufts of leaves and deep blue-purple flowers. There is also a pure white form. *S. atlanticum* (15cm; 6in) has slender leaves and masses of white starry flowers with a dark purple centre, and *S. depauperatum* is taller (23cm; 9in) with creamy flowers and a striking maroon eye. *S. californicum* (15cm; 6in) is well-known, with its fans of leaves and bright golden flowers, and its propensity for seeding everywhere. Remove seed-heads before they are ripe to control the spread of seedlings. *S. macrocarpon* has broad leaves and large flowers of rich golden yellow, spotted brown at the base, growing to 15cm (6in). It is reasonably hardy in very well-drained soil. All sisyrinchiums are easily divided by pulling clumps apart – each fan of leaves has its own roots.

Sisyrinchium macrocarpon

Soldanella

A small genus whose species have round leaves and beautiful, fringed, bell-shaped flowers. They require a moist, cool but open position, preferably in peaty soil, and will thrive in sun as long as the soil never dries out. They do not always flower freely, sometimes due to slug damage as the buds are formed in early winter and nestle at soil level. Overhead winter protection may also encourage better flowering. The alpine snowbell, *S. alpina* (8 × 10cm; 3 × 4in), has rounded, leathery, dark green leaves and deeply fringed, pendent, lavender flowers on very short stems, although you will find that it is shy-flowering in gardens. *S. villosa* is an easier, larger species with hairy leaf-stalks and 10–30cm (4–12in) stems of violet flowers, growing well on peat beds. *S. minima* is a tiny carpeter (2 × 10cm; 1 × 4in), with dark green leaves and pale violet or white, slightly fringed flowers.

Solidago

The goldenrods have leafy stems and dense heads of tiny, daisy-like flowers, and there are several miniature forms, easily grown on raised beds and gravel gardens to give late summer colour. *S. multiradiata* is a lovely, low-growing form making 10cm (4in) wide mats of deep green leaves with 10cm (4in) stems of congested golden-yellow flowers. Grow in groups for more impact. *S.* 'Queenie' (20cm; 8in) is a densely tufted goldenrod with leafy stems of golden foliage and pyramidal heads of bright golden flowers. *S. cutleri* makes neat, leafy tufts with short-stemmed golden-yellow clusters of flowers, reaching 15cm (6in). Propagate by seed or division.

Stachys

S. iva is a lovely dwarf species from Greece, with densely white-woolly grey leaves in neat tufts and bearing whorled spikes of cream flowers. Growing to 10 × 10cm (4 × 4in), it needs full sun and sharply drained gritty soil, and is ideal for troughs. *S. monieri* has dark green, crinkly leaves and delicate pink flower spikes on 15–20cm (6–8in) stems, and makes an attractive low mat of 20cm (8in) or more on a gravel or raised bed.

Tanacetum

Tanacetum densum subsp. *amani* is a beautiful low, mounded foliage plant that has soft, deeply dissected silvery grey leaves, growing 10–15cm (4–6in) high with a wider spread of 40–50cm (16–20in). The insignificant, yellowish flowers are best removed. Excellent with other sun-loving plants in gritty soil, providing a foil for brightly coloured flowers or a background for soft, pastel colours. It is perfectly hardy as long as sharp drainage is provided.

Teucrium

The germanders are interesting, fairly easy alpines for raised beds, gravel or troughs, many having aromatic foliage, and heads of lipped flowers. Propagate by cuttings. *T. chamaedrys* is well known, forming a 20cm (8in) wide bush of glossy, dark green leaves on 30cm (12in) upright stems and bearing leafy spikes of rose-pink flowers. Prune in spring to keep it bushy. It also makes a neat edging, responding well to clipping. *T. montanum* (8 × 20cm; 3¼ × 8in) grows into a tangled mat of leathery green leaves, white beneath, requiring regular trimming to keep it neat. The flowers are white ageing to cream and are surrounded by a ruff of leaves. *T. polium* (10–15cm; 4–6in) has downy, silvery green leaves that appear almost white, forming a low mat 15–20cm (6–8in) across, with heads of yellow flowers, and may not always survive in a wet winter. *T. ackermannii* (8 × 15cm; 3¼ × 6in) forms a spreading mat of aromatic, narrow grey-green foliage and bears heads of violet buds opening to rosy-purple flowers from mid to late summer.

Thalictrum

These are lovely little plants for growing in a peat bed or other partially shaded moist, leafy soil. They have fern-like, divided foliage, which dies down over winter, and sprays of small flowers with conspicuous stamens. The daintiest species is *T. kiusianum*, with neat finely divided foliage and wiry stems of tiny, pinkish-mauve flowers. Only 10cm (4in) high, it forms mildly spreading patches. *T. minus* has drooping, yellowish flowers on 20cm (8in) stems, and can be grown in drier soils. Plants may be divided in spring.

Thymus

There are several prostrate or bushy thymes, some with aromatic leaves, some coloured or variegated, all carrying heads of white, mauve or pink flowers beloved by bees. *T.* × *citriodorus* 'Golden Queen' (30 × 18cm; 12 × 7in) is an upright, bushy, lemon-scented form with green leaves edged gold, and *T. pulegioides* 'Aureus' and 'Archer's Gold' both have golden leaves on bushes about 15cm (6in) high. *T.* 'Doone Valley' is popular, with prostrate mats 20–30cm (8–12in) wide, bearing green and gold variegated leaves. *T.* 'Porlock' grows into a wide, low bush 15–20cm (6–8in) by up to 30cm (12in), bearing dark green, aromatic foliage and many, showy pink flowers. *T. herba-barona* grows into a tangled mat 30cm (12in) or more across, or can be allowed to trail, its thin stems covered in dark green caraway-scented leaves and heads of deep rose-purple flowers. *T. serpyllum*, a similarly sized prostrate mat of tiny leaves with many flowers, has several named forms, including var. *albus* (white, with bright green leaves), 'Annie Hall' (very pale pink), 'Pink Chintz' (clear pink, with olive green leaves) and 'Russetings' (deep pink). 'Elfin' is a tight dome of minute foliage, rarely exceeding 5 × 15cm (2 × 6in) and 'Minimus' a restrained prostrate mat 15cm (6in) across with woolly leaves and pinkish-mauve flowers. Both are suitable for troughs. Thyme cuttings root readily, and rooted pieces can be removed from prostrate forms.

Thymus **'Doone Valley'**

Townsendia

These have daisy-like flowers over neat rosettes of leaves, and are best grown in a trough with very sharp drainage. *T. formosa* (10cm; 4in) has large lilac, orange-centred flowers, while *T. incana* (3–5cm; 1–2in) forms a mat of grey-green leaves and has cream buds opening to white, pink-tinged flowers. *T. rothrockii* (7cm; 3in) has small, neat rosettes with lavender-violet flowers. They may be raised from seed, obtained from more specialist sources.

Veronica pectinata

Trollius

With their buttercup-like flowers and palmate leaves, these are attractive in sunny or partially shaded spots where the soil does not dry out, and may be raised from seed. Small alpine species, forming patches some 15cm (6in) across, include *T. acaulis* (12cm; 5in), with bright green, lobed leaves and wide open golden flowers, and *T. pumilus*, with three-lobed leaves and golden flowers on 15cm (6in) stems.

Veronica pinnata **'Blue Eyes'**

Veronica

There are many lovely species and cultivars of speedwell, all forming mats of foliage and bearing tapering spikes of flowers. *V. pectinata* has long, trailing stems, spreading 30cm (12in) or more, clothed in deeply cut, small leaves and short spikes of bright blue flowers. *V. prostrata* forms a prostrate mat, up to 30cm (12in) or more wide, with royal-blue flowers, and the many named forms include 'Blue Sheen' (soft milky blue), 'Mrs Holt' (soft pink) and 'Trehane' (bright blue, with golden leaves). 'Nana' is a tiny form with little blue flowers, ideal for troughs. *V. peduncularis* 'Georgia Blue' (15 × 30cm; 6 × 12in) makes

hummocks of bronzed leaves carrying rich blue, white-eyed flowers. *V. austriaca* subsp. *teucrium* 'Royal Blue' (20 × 30cm; 8 × 12in or more) has long spikes of deep blue flowers, while *V. austriaca* 'Ionian Skies' (15 × 15cm; 6 × 6in) has beautiful sky-blue spikes over low tufts of delicate toothed leaves. *V. spicata* 'Heidekind' (20 × 20cm; 8 × 8in) forms low mounds of leaves and tapering deep pink flower spikes, and *V. pinnata* 'Blue Eyes' has deeply cut leaves and spikes of light blue flowers on 15–20cm (6–8in) stems. Propagate veronicas by softwood or semi-ripe cuttings, or in some cases from seed.

Viola hederacea

Viola

Violets are lovely additions to alpine plantings, flowering for a long period and thriving in partially shaded positions. Here are just a few suggestions, all forming clumps 15–25cm (6–10in) or more across. *V. cornuta* 'Alba Minor' grows to 20cm (8in), each white flower having a long pointed spur behind it. *V. pedata*, the bird's-foot violet, has deeply lobed leaves in 12cm (5in) tufts, with reddish-purple flowers in spring. *V. hederacea* (8cm; 3in) is attractive, but really hardy only in mild areas, with trailing stems of kidney-shaped leaves and mauve flowers tipped with white borne on long stalks from mid-summer. *V. verecunda* var. *yakusimana* is an extremely tiny Japanese violet, 3cm (1in) in height at the most, with minute heart-shaped leaves and tiny white, purple-veined flowers in early to mid-summer. Grow it in a partially shaded trough or pan.

There are many violas of garden origin, in a huge range of colours, including 'Moonlight' (soft creamy yellow with yellow eye), 'Milkmaid' (palest blue fading to white) and 'Molly Sanderson' (satiny, almost black). Many violas can be raised from seed.

Acknowledgements

The authors are grateful to the following for allowing them to photograph their plants and gardens: Kathryn Allen; Gerry & Margaret Elliott; Cliff & Pat Jarrett; Derek Richardson; John & Betty Wheeler.

About the authors

Chris and Valerie Wheeler own a nursery
specializing in dwarf plants, including alpines.
They design and provide plants for alpine features,
and also run gardening courses through the Suffolk
Garden School. They are the authors of *Gardening
with Hebes* and *Sink & Container Gardening using Dwarf
and Hardy Plants*, both published by GMC.

INDEX

Page numbers in **bold** refer to illustrations

A
'Abbotswood' (*Potentilla*) **97**
Acer 14
Achillea 86, 87, 98
  chrysocoma 98
  'Huteri' 18, 21, 24, 51, **86**, 87, 91, **98**
  × *lewisii*
    'King Edward' 20, 98
acid lovers 32
Acinos
  alpinus **16**, 51, **99**
Aethionema 51, 99
  armenum **99**
  grandiflorum 99
  'Warley Rose' 99
AGS *see* Alpine Garden Society
Alchemilla (lady's mantle) 100
  alpina 100
  ellenbeckii 100
  erythropoda **100**
'Alix Brett' (*Aubrieta*) 105
Allium
  beesianum 24
  callimischon 24
  cernuum 24
alpine
  definition 3–4
  types 4
alpine avens (*Geum Montanum*) 114
alpine candytuft (*Iberis*) 116
  aurosiaca
    'Sweetheart' **116**

sempervirens 116
  'Schneeflocke' 92, 116
  'Weisser Zwerg' 116
Alpine Garden Society (AGS) 28, 29, 112
alpine house 3, **12**, 28
alpine snowbell (*Soldanella alpina*) 134
Alyssum 100
  serpyllifolium 27, **100**
  spinosum
    'Roseum' 16, 21, **78**, **100**
'Amazing Grace' (*Phlox*) **20**, 62, 123
American Rock Garden Society 28
Anacyclus (Mount Atlas daisy) 16, 100
  pyrethrum 7, **16**, **62**, 100
Andes 41
Androsace (rock jasmine) 101
  carnea 101
  laggeri 101
  lanuginosa 101
  sempervivoides 101
Anemone 42, 43, 101
  caroliniana 18, 61, 101
  × *lesseri* 101
  nemorosa (wood anemone) 4, 101
    'Robinsoniana' 101
    'Vestal' 101
  sylvestris 101
'Angel's Wings' (*Gentiana*) 112
'Annie Hall' (*Thymus*) 136
annuals 4
Antennaria 51, 101
  microphylla 101, **21**
  parvifolia 101
Anthemis
  marschalliana 21, 102

Antirrhinum
  sempervirens 102
ants 39
aphids 37
Aquilegia 42, 102
  bertonii 102
  flabellata
    'Ministar' 51, 102
  laramiensis 61, 102
Arabis 102
  alpina
    'Flore-Pleno' 102
    'Pink Pearl' 102
    'Rosea' 102
  ferdinandi-coburgii
    'Old Gold' **17**, 18, 102
    'Variegata' 102
'Archer's Gold' (*Thymus*) 24, 136
Arenia 102
  montana 102
  purpurasens 102, **103**
  tetraquetra 102
Armeria 35, 59, 90, 103
  juniperifolia 24, 73, 103
    'Alba' **103**
    'Beechwood' 103
    'Bevan's Variety' 61, 103
  maritima **91**
    'Alba' 103
    'Düsseldorfer Stolz' 103
    'Splendens' 92, **93**, **103**
    'Vindictive' 93, 103
Artemisia 51, 103
  caucasica 103
  schmidtiana
    'Nana' 103
Aruncus 17

aethusifolius (goat's beard) 51, **64**, 104

Asperula 51, 104

   gussonei 16, 27, 61, 73, **78**, 90, 104

   lilaciflora **104**

Asplenum

   trichomanes

      'Incisum' 24

Aster

   alpinus 6, 18, **59**, 104

      'Pinkie' 104

      'Trimix' **104**

   nova-belgii

      'Jenny' **97**

Aubrieta 18, 39, 90, 105

   'Alix Brett' 105

   'Aureovariegata' 18, 105

   'Doctor Mules' 105

   'Royal Red' 105

   'Royal Violet' 105

Aurinia

   saxatilis (gold dust) 105

      'Citrina' 105

      'Dudley Nevill' 105

      'Goldkugel' 105

Australasia 127

B

'Badenoch (*Cassiope*) **64**

'Bagatelle (*Berberis*) 24

'Ballerina' (*Geranium*) 113

bark chippings 32, 58, 70

basket liners 76

'Beechpark red' (*Helianthemum*) 7

'Beechwood' (*Armeria*) 103

bees 37

Bellium

   minutum **94**, 105

'Ben Fhada' (*Helianthemum*) 114

'Ben Ledi' (*Helianthemum*) 21, 77, 93, 114

Berberis

   × *stenophylla*

      'Corallina Compacta' **23**, 24, **62**

   thunbergii

      'Bagatelle' 24

      'Dart's Red Lady' **97**

'Kobold' 24

'Berlin Snow' (*Dianthus*) 16, 27, 73, **78**, 108

Betula

   nana **64**

'Bevan's Variety' (*Armeria*) 61, 103

'Bewerley White' (*Primula*) 125

biological controls 37, 38, 39

'Birch Hybrid' (*Campanula*) **21**, 51, **61**, **62**, 90, **91**, 106

bird's-eye primrose (*Primula farinosa*) **64**, 125

bird's foot violet (*Viola pedata*) 138

'Bishop's Form' (*Erodium*) 10, 27, **86**, **111**

'Black Knight' (*Sempervivum*) 132

'Blau Saphir' (*Linum*) 51, **119**

'Blaue Clips' (*Campanula*) 106

'Blaulicht' (*Jasione*) 117

'Blue Boy' (*Sempervivum*) 132

'Blue Dream' (*Chaenorhinum*) 107

'Blue Eyes' (*Veronica*) **62**, **137**

'Blue Sheen' (*Veronica*) 61, **62**, 137

borders 13, 21, 90-93, 98, 108, 116, 122, 125

   plant selection 92–3

   planting scheme **96–7**

Botrytis (grey mould) **36**, 49

'Boydii' (*Salix*) 24

brick rubble 57

bricks 55

'Brilliant' (*Dianthus*) 108

Britain 4

'Buckland' (*Origanum*) 73, 120, **121**

bulbs 15, 22, 24, 35, 39, 59

bushy plants 7, 18

buying seeds 41

C

'Caerulea' (*Primula*) 125

Calceolaria 87, 105

   'John Innes' 27, **64**, 105

   polyrrhiza 105

   tenella 61, **64**, 105

Campanula 4, 34, 39, 51, 59, 106

   'Birch Hybrid' **21**, 51, **61**, **62**, 90, **91**, 106

   carpatica 106

      'Blaue Clips' 106

'Chewton Joy' 106

cochleariifolia 106

   'Elizabeth Oliver' 21, 27, **106**

garganica 24, 87, **94**, 106

   'Blue Diamond' 106

   'Dickson's Gold' 106

'Hallii' 106

persicifolia

   'Chettle Charm' **97**

porscharskyana 91, 92, 106

   'E. H. Frost' 106

   'Lisduggan Variety' 106

   'Stella' 21, 93, 106

pulla 106

'Cangshan' (*Gentiana*) 112

'Cape Blanco' (*Sedum*) 131

'Carnival' (*saxifraga*) 128

Cassiope 24, 61

   'Badenoch' **64**

   'Edinburgh' **64**

catalogues 27

cats 39

Chaenorhinum

   origanifolium **94**, **107**

      'Blue Dream' 107

Chamaecyparis

   lawsoniana

      'Gnome' 23

'Chettle Charm' (*Campanula*) **97**

'Chewton Joy' (*Campanula*) 106

Chiastophyllum 17, 90

   oppositifolium **10**, 91, **107**

      'Jim' s Pride' 107

China 112

chippings 13

'Christine' (*Primula*) 124

'Citrina' (*Aurinia*) 105

'Clarence Elliott' (*Saxifraga*) 61, 128

cleaning seeds 42–3

'Cloth of Gold' (*Saxifraga*) 128

coastal plants 4

cobweb houseleek (*Sempervivum arachnoideum*) 132

cold frame 37, **44**, 47, 71

colour 5, 19-21

'Colwall' (*Hebe*) 24

'Commander Hay' (*Sempervivum*) 132

compost 44, 45, 46, 49, 70, 77, 88

conditions required 3–4

conifers 22, 23–4, 59, 71, 85, 90
containers *see also* troughs 24, 34, 36, 39, 47, **60**, 67–81, 86, 107, 108, 122, 129, 138
  maintenance 72
  plant selection 70–71
  planting 71–2, 76–7
  suitable plants 73
Convolvulus
  lineatus 16, 18, 27, **62**, 107
'Corallina Compacta (*Berberis*) **23**, 24, **62**
Corsican mint (*Mentha requienii*) 119
'Country Park' (*Pratia*) 124
'Crackerjack' (*Phlox*) 24, **123**
cracks 89
creeping alpines 89
crocuses 24
Cryptomeria
  japonica
    'Compressa' 23–4
cushion forming plants 6, 19, 72, 87
cuttings 46–9, 51
Cyclamen **44**
  coum 24
  hederifolium 24
Cyclamen Society 28

D
'Dainty Dame' (*Dianthus*) 24, 61, 108, **62**
'Dali (*Gentiana*) 61, 112
Daphne 24
'Dart's Red Lady' **97**
dead-heading 34, 35, 84
'Delight' (*Parahebe*) 24, 77, 122
'Dewdrop' (*Dianthus*) 77, **97**, 108
'Diamant' (*Linum*) 119
Dianthus 16, 18, 32, 51, 59, 77, **86**, 108
  alpinus 108
    'Joan's Blood' 108, **81**
  'Berlin Snow' 16, 27, 73, **78**, 108
  callizonus **61**, 108
  'Dainty Dame' 24, 61, **62**, 108
  deltoides 51, 108
    'Albus' 108
    'Brilliant' 108

'Dewdrop' 77, **97**, 108
'La Bourboule' 24, **81**, 108
'Nyewood's Cream' **81**, 108
petraeus **81**, 108
'Whatfield Joy' 24, **62**, 73, **108**
'Whatfield Magenta' 108
'Whatfield Wisp' 21, 24, **81**, 108
Diascia 87, 108
  barbarae
    'Ruby Field' 108
  integerrima 108
  'Lilac Belle' 108
  lilacina 108
disabled and elderly 53, 54
division **50**
'Doctor Mules' (*Aubrieta*) 105
Dodecatheon (shooting stars) 17, 87, 109
  dentatum **64**, 109
  meadia **61**, 109
  pulchellum **64**, 109
'Doone Valley' (*Thymus*) **20**, 94, **136**
double walls 90
'Dr Hahnle' (*Erinus*) 110
'Dr Ramsey' (*Saxifraga*) 128
Draba 6, 35, 109
  aizoides 109
  rigida 109
drainage 13, 32, 53, 58, 84
drainage materials 57, 69
drought 36
drumstick primrose (*Primula denticulata*) 24, 125
Dryas (mountain avens) 109
  octopetala 109
    'Minor' 109
Dryopteris
  erythrosa
    'Prolifera' 24
'Dubia' (*Gypsophila*) 77, 114
'Dudley Nevill' (*Aurinia*) 105
'Düsseldorfer Stolz' (*Armeria*) 103
dwarf irises **16**

E
'E. H. Frost' (*Campanula*) 106
edelweiss (*Leontopodium alpinum*) 117

'Mignon' 117
'Edinburgh' (*Cassiope*) **64**
'Edith sarah' (*Gentiana*) 112
'Elfin' (*Thymus*) 6, 73, 136
'Elizabeth Oliver' (*Campanula*) 21, 27, **106**
envelopes 43
Epilobium (willowherb)
  crassum 17, 51, 109
ericaceous compost 70
ericaceous plants 56, 58, 61, 70
Erigeron 110
  acer debilis 110
  alpinus 110
  compositus 16, 21, 61, **62**, **110**
  'Four Winds' 110
Erinus 16
  alpinus **6**, **62**, 90, 110
    'Albus' 110
    'Dr Hahnle' 110
    'Mrs Charles Boyle' 110
Erodium 17, 39, 51, 59, 111
  chrysanthum **59**, 111
  guttatum 111
  reichardii 111
  × *variabile*
    'Bishop's Form' 10, 27, **86**, **111**
    'Flore Pleno' **78**, 111
'Esther' (*Saxifraga*) 128
Europe 4
European Alps 4
'Eva Constance' (*Pulsatilla*) **91**, 126
evergreens 59

F
'Faldonside' (*Primula*) 125
farmyard manure 32
feeding 34, 59, 77, 85, 88
ferns 22, 24
fertilizer 49, 59
flax (*Linum*) 119
  'Gemmell's Hybrid' 61, 119
  perenne
    'Blau Saphir' 51, **119**
    'Diamant' 119
flowering season 10
'Four Winds' (*Erigeron*) 110

Frankenia 34, 87
   thymifolia 61, 111
'Fratensis' (*Gypsophila*) 21, 24, 73, 114
front of border 24

G
'Gaiety' (*Saxifraga*) 128
garden compost 32
'Gemmell's Hybrid' (*Linum*) 61, 119
Genista 24
Gentiana 4, 27, 112
   acaulis (trumpet gentian) 4, 27, **45**, 51, **112**
   saxosa 112
   septemfida 20, 27, 61, 112
   sino-ornata **64**, 112
      'Alba' 112
      'Angel's Wings' 112
      'Edith Sarah' 112
      'Mary Lyle' 61, 112
   ternifolia 112
      'Cangshan' 112
      'Dali' 61, 112
   verna 112
'Georgia Blue' (*Veronica*) 137
Geranium 17, 49, 59, **77**, 113
   cinereum **113**
      'Ballerina' 113
      'Laurence Flatman' **97**, **113**
   dalmaticum 78, 113
   sanguineum **17**, 24, 77, 91, 92, 113
      'Album' 113
      'Max Frei' 113
   sessiliflorum
      'Nigricans' 113
germander (*Teucrium*) 135
   ackermannii 135
   chamaedrys 135
   montanum 135
   polium 135
germination 43
Geum 10, 114
   montanum (alpine avens) 114
   pentapetalum 61, 114
glazed sinks **67**
glyphosphate 54, 84

'Gnome' (*Chamaecyparis*) 23
goat's beard (*Aruncus aethusifolius*) 51, **64**, 104
gold dust (*Aurinia saxatilis*) 105
   'Citrina' 105
   'Dudley Nevill' 105
   'Goldkugel' 105
'Golden Queen' (*Thymus*) 136
golden thyme **87**
goldenrod (*Solidago*) 18, 59, 134
   cutleri 134
   multiradiata **18, 62**, 134
   'Queenie' 134
'Goldkugel' (*Aurinia*) 105
'Goldstream' (*Thymus*) 87
'Grace Ward' (*Lithodora*) 119
gravel 57
gravel beds 21, 24, 27, **82**–6, 98, 103, 108, 110, 116, 119, 121, 122, 134
   maintenance 84–5
   plant selection 85-6
   planting 84
   preparation 83–4
Greece 134
'Greencourt White' (*Hypsela*) 115
greenhouse 36–7, 44, 71
grey mould *see Botrytis*
'Grigg's Surprise' (*Sempervivum*) 132
grit 13, 32, 39, 44, 57–8, 84, 92
ground cover 100, 101, 103, 122
growing conditions 12–13, 15
growth habit 6–10
Gypsophila 34, 87, 114
   aretioides 114
      'Caucasica' 114
   cerastioides 114
   repens 7, 114
      'Dubia' 77, 114
      'Fratensis' 21, 24, 73, 114
      'Rosea' 114
      white form **114**

H
habitats 3–4
'Hallii' (*Campanula*) 106
hanging baskets 76, **77**
hardcore 88
hardiness 11

'Heavenly Blue' (*Lithodora*) 119
heavy soils 32, 92
Hebe
   'Colwall' 24
   'Heidi' **97**
   'Jasper' 24
   raoulii 24
'Heidekind' (*Veronica*) 137
'Heidi' (*Hebe*) **97**
Helianthemum (rock roses) 4, 5, 7, 16, 18, 34, 35, 61, 86, 89, 114
   'Beechpark Red' **7**
   'Ben Fhada' 114
   'Ben Ledi' 21, 77, 93, 114
   lunulatum 114
   oelandicum **73**, 114
   'Sterntaler' 20, 24, **94**
   'Sudbury Gem' **97**, 114
   'The Bride' 114
   'Wisley Primrose' 24, 114
Helichrysum
   bellidioides 115
hen-and-chicken houseleek (*Jovibarba sobolifera*) 117
herbaceous perennials 4, 15
herbicides 54
high pastures 4
Himalayas 41
'Hokkaido' (*Ulmus*) 24
hybridiation 42
Hypericum 86, 115
   cerastioides **20**, **115**
   empetrifolium subsp. *tortuosum* 61, 115
   olympicum 7, 18, 20, 24, 51, 115
      'Sulphureum' 115
   reptans 7, **87**
hypertufa 67-68, 68
Hypsela
   reniformis 115
      'Greencourt White' 115
Hyssopus 34

I
Iberis (alpine candytuft) 116
   aurosiaca
      'Sweetheart' **116**
   sempervirens 116
      'Schneeflocke' 92, 116

'Weisser Zwerg' 116
'Iceberg' (*Phlox*) 123
Ilex
    crenata 24
'Imperial Gem' (*Lavandula*) 97
insecticides 37, 38, 39
'Incisum' (*Asplenum*) 24
'Ionian Skies' (*Veronica*) 137
Ionopsidium
    acaule 4, **116**
Iris 24, **86**
    reticulata **25**
'Iris Prichard' (*Saxifraga*) 128

J
Japan 138
Jasione 117
    heldreichii 117
    laevis 117
        'Blaulicht' 117
'Jasper' (*Hebe*) 24
'Jenkinsiae' (*Saxifraga*) 128, **129**
'Jenny' (*Aster*) **97**
'Jim's Pride (*Chiastophyllum*) 107
'Joan's Blood' (*Dianthus*) **81**, 108
'John Innes' (*Calceolaria*) 27, **64**, 105
Jovibarba 117
    arenaria 73, 117
    hirta 117
    sobolifera (hen-and-chickens
        houseleek) 117
'Julie-Anne' (*Parahebe*) 61, 93, **97**,
    122
Juniperus
    communis
        'Compressa' 23, **70**

K
Kalmiopsis 24, 61
'King George' (*Sempervivum*) **62**, **132**
'Kobold' 24

L
'La Bourboule' (*Dianthus*) 24, **81**,
    108
ladybirds 37
lady's mantle (*Alchemilla*) 100
    alpina 100
    ellenbeckii 100

erythropoda **100**
'Laurence Flatman' (*Geranium*) **97**,
    113
Lavandula 24
    angustifolia
        'Imperial Gem' **97**
leaf colour 10, 17–18
leaf mould 58
leaf shape 10
Leontopodium 117
    alpinum (edelweiss) 117
        'Mignon' 117
Leptinella 51, 117
    potentillina 89, 117
    squalida 117
Leucojum 24
Lewisia 17, 39, 42, 75, 90, 118
    cantelovii 118
    columbiana 118
    cotyledon **5**, **40**, 51, **74**, 90, **118**
    'George Henley' 118
    nevadensis 118
    pygmaea 118
'Lilac Belle' (*Diascia*) 108
lime haters 70
lime lovers 32
'Limelight' (*Sempervivum*) 132
limestone chippings 32
Limonium (statice) 16, 59, 118
    bellidifolium 21, 73, **62**, 118
    cosyrense 73, 118
    gougetianum 118
    minutum **78**, 118
Linum (flax) 119
    'Gemmell's Hybrid' 61, 119
    perenne
        'Blau Saphir' 51, **119**
        'Diamant' 119
'Lisduggan variety' (*Campanula*) 106
Lithodora 119
    diffusa 27, 119
        'Alba' 119
        'Grace Ward' 119
        'Heavenly Blue' 119
    oleifolia 119
loam 57
logs 56
London pride (*Saxifraga* × *urbium*)
    51, 88, 128

'Clarence Elliott' 61, 128

M
mail order 27
maintenance
    gravel beds 84–5
    raised beds 59
    troughs 72
'Mary Lyle' (*Gentiana*) 61, 112
'Max Frei' (*Geranium*) 113
'McDaniel's Cushion' (*Phlox*) 123
meadows 4
Mediterranean 4
Mentha
    requienii (Corsican mint) 119
'Mersea Yellow' (*Penstemon*) 122
mice 39
'Mignon' (*Leonopodium*) 117
'Milkmaid' (*Viola*) 138
miniature landscapes 71
'Ministar' (*Aquilegia*) 51, 102
Minuartia 6, 120
    circassica **16**, 21, 61, **62**, **120**
    stellata 16, 27, 73, 120
Mitella 120
    breweri **64**, **120**
    caulescens 61, 120
    diphylla 120
moisture lovers 87
'Molly Sanderson' (*Viola*) 138
'Moonlight' (*Viola*) 138
moss 89
mound forming plants *see* cushion
    forming plants
Mount Atlas daisy (*Anacyclus*) 16,
    100
    pyrethrum 7, **16**, **62**
'Mount Snowdon' (*Silene*) 73, 133
mountain avens (*Dryas*) 109
    octopetala 109
        'Minor' 109
mountain plants 4
mountainous regions 4
mousetraps 39, **45**
'Mrs Charles Boyle (*Erinus*) 110
'Mrs Giuseppi' (*Sempervivum*) 132
'Mrs Helen Terry' (*Saxifraga*) 128
'Mrs Holt' (*Veronica*) **86**, 137
'Myra' (*Saxifraga*) 128

N

narcissi 24
nematodes 38, 39
New Zealand 112
New Zealand Alpine Garden
    Society 28
newsletters and journals 29
'Nigricans' (*Geranium*) 113
'Nigrum' (*Sempervivum*) 132
Northern Hemisphere 4
nurseries 7
'Nyewood's Cream' (*Dianthus*) 81,
    108

O

offsets 51, 117, 118
'Old Gold' (*Arabis*) **17**, 18, 102
'Old Yellow Dusty Miller' (*Primula*)
    125
organic matter 32
Origanum 120
    'Buckland' 73, 120, **121**
    microphyllum 7, 21, 61, 120
    rotundifolium 120
Oxalis 121
    adenophylla **31**, **62**, **121**
    enneaphylla 121
        'Rosea' 121
    magellanica 89, 121

P

'Pacino' (*Papaver*) 121
Papaver (poppy) 16, 87, 121
    alpinum 51, **94**, 121
    miyabeanum
        'Pacino' 121
    rupifragrum 121
'Paradise Yellow' (*Primula*) 125
Parahebe 4, 59, 77, 122
    catarractae
        'Delight' 24, 77, 122
        'Rosea' 122
    lyallii 24, 90, **122**
        'Julie-Anne' 61, 93, **97**, 122
pasque flower (*Pulsatilla*) 43, 46,
    59, **91**, 126
    vernalis 126
    vulgaris **60**, **97**, 126
        'Alba' **126**

'Eva Constance' **91**, 126
patios 87–8
paving 15, 86–7, 91, 101, 116,
    117, 119, 121, 124
    planting 89
    planting scheme **94–5**
'Pearly King' (*Saxifraga*) 128
peat 46, 58
peat beds 15, 22, 24, 27, 61,
    64–5, 107, 109, 114, 124, 125,
    135
peat blocks 56–7
pelleted poultry manure 34, 59,
    85, 88
Penstemon 122
    fruticosus 122
    newberryi 122
    pinifolius 4, 20, 24, 51, 61, 122
        'Mersea Yellow' 122
        'Wisley Flame' 91, **62**, 122
    'Pink Dragon' 122
    'Six Hills' 122
Persicaria 10, 18, 34, 59
    vaccinifolia 4, **62**, 122, **123**
pests and pest control 37–9
Phlox 16, 18, 34, 59, 123
    douglasii 24, 73, 123
        'Crackerjack' 24, **123**
        'Iceberg' 123
        'Red Admiral' **78**, 123
        'Rosea' 24, **73**, 123
        'Violet Queen' 24, 123
    kelseyi
        'Rosette' 123
    × *procumbens*
        'Variegata' 123
    subulata 123
        'Amazing Grace' **20**, **62**, 123
        'McDaniel's Cushion' 123
        'Temiskaming' 123
Phyllodoce 24
Phyteuma 6, 123
    hemisphaericum 123
    scheuchzeri 20, 61, **62**, **123**
'Pink Chintz' (*Thymus*) 136
'Pink Dragon' (*Penstemon*) 122
'Pink Pearl' (*Arabis*) 102
'Pinkei (*Aster*) 104
plant centres 27

plant selection
    borders 92–3
    gravel areas 85–6
    pond surrounds 87
    troughs 70–71
plant shapes and habit 6–10,
    18–19
planting 32–3, 76–7
    cracks 89
    gravel beds 84
    patio 88
    paving 89
    steps 89
    troughs 71–2
    walls 90
planting schemes
    border edge 96–7
    containers 78–81
    paving **94–5**
    peat beds **64–5**
    raised beds 59–61, **62–3**
Polystichum
    setiferum
        'Congestum' 24
pond surrounds 86–7
poppy (*Papaver*) 16, 87
    alpinum 51, **94**, 121
    miyabeanum
        'Pacino' 121
    rupifragrum 121
'Porlock' (*Thymus*) 24, **91**, 136
position 31
Potentilla 124
    cuneata 124
    eriocarpa **62**, 124
    fruticosa
        'Abbotswood' **97**
    nitida 61, 124
    × *tonguei* **91**, 124
pots 15
Pratia 89, 124
    angulata 124
        'Treadwellii' 124
    pedunculata 124
        'Country Park' 124
Primula 18, 46, 59, 87
    auricula 125
        'Old Yellow Dusty Miller' 125
        'Paradise Yellow' 125

denticulata (drumstick primrose) 24, 125

farinosa (bird's-eye primrose) **64**, 125

frondosa 61, **64**, 125

marginata 125
    'Caerulea' 125
    × *pubescens* 125
        'Bewerley White' 125
        'Boothman's Variety' 125
        'Christine' **124**
        'Faldonside' 125

reidii 125

'Prince Hal' (*Saxifraga*) **18**, 128

propagator 48

prostrate plants 7, 70, 72

pruning 34–36

Pterocephalus 59
    perennis 16, 27, 51, 90, 125

Pulsatilla (pasque flower) 43, 46, 59, 126
    vernalis 126
    vulgaris **60**, **97**, 126
        'Alba' **126**
        'Eva Constance' **91**, 126

'Purpurteppich' (*Sedum*) 60, 62, 131

puschkinias 24

'Pygmalion' (*Saxifraga*) 128

Q

'Queenie' (*Solidago*) 134

R

railway sleepers 55

raised beds 13, 15, 21, 22, 24, 27, 34, 39, **52**, 53–64, 102, 103, 107, 108, 109, 114, 116, 120, 129, 134
    advantages 53
    building 54–7
    drainage material 57
    filling 57–8
    maintenance 59
    planting schemes 59
    position 54
    size and shape 53–4
    soil 57–8
    top dressing 58

Ranunculus 126

crenatus 126

gramineus 20, **126**

Raoulia 127
    australia 127
    haastii 127
    hookeri 127

reconstituted stone 55

'Red Admiral' (*Phlox*) **78**, 123

'Red Devil' (*Sempervivum*) **132**

retaining walls 55, 90

Rhododendron 24, 61
    impeditum **64**

'Robinsoniana' (*Anemone*) 101

rock gardens 12, 31

rock jasmine (*Androsace*) 101
    carnea 101
    laggeri 101
    lanuginosa 101
    sempervivoides 101

rock plants 4

rock roses (*Helianthemum*) 4, 5, 7, 16, 18, 34, 35, 61, 86, 89
    'Beechpark Red' 7
    'Ben Fhada' 114
    'Ben Ledi' 21, 77, 93, 114
    lunulatum 114
    oelandicum **73**, 114
    'Sterntaler' 20, 24, **94**
    'Sudbury Gem' **97**, 114
    'The Bride' 114
    'Wisley Primrose' 24, 114

rocks 70, 83, 86

root aphids **38**

root cuttings 46, 49

rooting compound 48

'Rosenteppich' (*Saponaria*) 127

roses 91, 93

'Rosette' (*Phlox*) 123

rosettes 18, 35, 37, 47, 118

'Royal Blue' (*Veronica*) 93, 137

'Royal Red' (*Aubrieta*) 105

'Royal Violet' (*Aubrieta*) 105

'Royanum' (*Sempervivum*) 132

'Ruby Field' (*Diascia*) 108

'Ruby Glow' (*Sedum*) **97**, 131

'Russetings (*Thymus*) 77, **94**, 136

S

Salix

'Boydii' 24

retusa **64**

serpyllifolia 24

sandy soils 32

Saponaria 4, 127
    ocymoides (tumbling Ted) 7, 51, 90, 127
    'Snow Tip' **74**, 127
    × *olivana* 127
    'Rosenteppich' 127

saving seeds 41-2

Saxifraga 5, **9**, **14**, 18, **30**, 32, 35, 37, 39, 47, 59, **60**, 71, 74, **83**, 90, 128
    × *anglica*
        'Myra' 128
    × *burnatii*
        'Dr Ramsey' 128
        'Esther' 128
    burseriana
        'Prince Hal' **18**, 128
    'Carnival' 128
    cochlearis
        'Minor' 128
    exarata
        'Cloth of Gold' 128
    'Gaiety' 128
    × *hardingii*
        'Iris Prichard' 128
    × *irvingii*
        'Jenkinsiae' 128, **129**
    'Pearly King' 128
    × *salmanica*
        'Mrs Helen Terry' 128
    × *urbium* (London pride) 51, **88**, 128
        'Clarence Elliott' 61, 128
    × *webriii*
        'Pygmalion' 128
    'Whitehill' 128
    'Winifred Bevington' **22**, 51, 128

Scabiosa 59, 86, 129
    graminifolia 129
    japonica 18, **62**, **129**

'Schneeflocke' (*Iberis*) 92, 116

scillas 24

Scleranthus
    biflorus 129
    uniflorus 129

Scottish Rock Garden Club 28
Scutellaria 4, 16, 51, 59, 86, 130
   alpina **97**, 130
   orientalis 130
   pontica **130**
   prostrata 130
   scordiifolia 130
seasonal interest 17-18, 59
Sedum 18, 34, 36, 59, **77**, 90, 91,
   131
   kamtschaticum **35**, **59**, **131**
      'Weihenstephaner Gold' 24,
        92, **97**, 131
   oreganum 10, 20, **62**, **131**
   'Ruby Glow' **97**, 131
   'Silver Moon' **131**
   spathulifolium **6**, **46**
      'Cape Blanco' 131
   spurium 24, 51, 77, 131
      'Purpurteppich' **60**, **62**, 131
      'Variegatum' **11**, 131
seed collecting expeditions 41
seed exchange schemes 41
seedlings 45
seeds 51
semi-ripe cuttings 46, 48
Sempervivum 10, 17, 18, **19**, 24, **26**,
   34, 35, 36, 39, 51, 59, 71, 73,
   74, 76, **83**, 86, 90, 117, 132
   arachnoideum (cobweb houseleek)
      132
   'Black Knight' 132
   'Blue Boy' 132
   calcareum 132
      'Grigg's Surprise' 132
      'Limelight' 132
      'Mrs Giuseppi' 132
   'Commander Hay' 132
   'Corsair' **78**
   'King George' **62**, **132**
   kosaninii 132
   'Red Devil' **132**
   tectorum 132
      'Nigrum' 132
      'Royanum' 132
   'Video' 132
shade 31
shade lovers 4, 17, 31
sharp sand 32

shooting stars (*Dodecatheon*) 17, 87,
   109
   dentatum **64**, 109
   meadia **61**, 109
   pulchellum **64**, 109
shows 28
shrubby alpines 18
shrubs 15, 22, 24, 59, 85, 90
sieves 42–3
Silene 133
   acaulis 4, 27, 51, 133
      'Mount Snowdon' 73, 133
   alpestris 133
      'Flore Pleno' **62**
'Silver Moon' (*Sedum*) **131**
sinks *see* troughs
Sisyrinchium 16, 18, 42, 51, 133
   atlanticum 133
   californicum 133
   depauperatum 133
   idahoense 21, **50–51**, 73, **133**
      'Album' **78**
   macrocarpon 27, **133**
'Six Hills' (*Penstemon*) 122
slug pellets 45
slug traps 39, 45
slugs and snails 29, 45
'Snow Tip' (*Saponaria*) **74**, 127
societies 28, 41
soft soap 37
softwood cuttings 46, **47–8**
soil 32, 57
soil type 13, 15
Soldanella 4, 27, 134
   alpina (alpine snowbell) 134
   minima 134
   villosa **61**, **64**, 134
Solidago (goldenrod) 18, 59, 134
   cutleri 134
   multiradiata **18**, **62**, 134
   'Queenie' 134
sources of plants 27
sowing seeds 44
Spain 121
Spiraea 24
   betulifolia **97**
'Splendens' 92, **93**, **103**
Stachys 134
   iva 21, 73, 134

   monieri 134
statice (*Limonium*) 16, 59, 118
   bellidifolium 21, **62**, 73
   cosyrense 73
   minutum **78**
'Stella' (*Campanula*) 21, 93, 106
steps 89
'Sterntaler' (*Helianthemum*) 20, 24, **94**
Stipa
   tenuissima **97**
stone 56
strawberry pots 75
'Sudbury Gem' (*Helianthemum*) **97**,
   114
sun 31
sun lovers 4, **14**, 16, 31
sun scorch 37, 45
'Sweetheart' (*Iberis*) **116**

T
Tanacetum 135
   densum 21, 86, 135
'Temiskaming' (*Phlox*) 123
terracotta pots 74–5
Teucrium (germander) 135
   ackermannii 135
   chamaedrys 135
   montanum 135
   polium 135
Thalictrum 135
   kiusianum 61, **64**, 135
   minus 135
'The Bride' (*Helinthemum*) 114
Thuja
   occidentalis
      'Caespitosa' 23
Thymus 16, 18, 34, 51, **86**, 87, 90,
   91, 136
   × *citriodorus* 7
      'Golden Queen' 136
   'Doone Valley' **20**, **94**, **136**
   herba-barona 136
   'Porlock' 24, 91, 136
   pulegioides
      'Archer's Gold' 24, 136
      'Aureus' 136
   serpyllum 7, 50, 136
      albus 136
      'Annie Hall' 136

'Elfin' 6, 73, 136
'Goldstream' 87
'Minimus' 24, 73, 136
'Pink Chintz' 136
'Russetings' 77, **94**, 136
Tiarella
wherryi **64**
timber 56, **57**
tomato fertilizer 49, 77
top dressing **13**, 32, 33, 39, 58, 59, 70, 72, 88, **92**
Townsendia 51, 136
formosa 136
incana 136
rothrockii 136
trailing plants 70, 87, 89
'Treadwellii' (*Pratia*) 124
tree trunks 76
'Trehane' (*Veronica*) 137
'Trimix' (*Aster*) **104**
trimming 34–6
Trollius 137
acaulis 137
pumilus **64**, 137
troughs *see also* containers 13, 15, 21, 22, 24, 27, **66**, 102, 103, 109, 120, 130, 131, 135, 137
filling **69–70**
maintenance 72
plant selection 70-71, 73
trumpet gentian (*Gentiana acaulis*) 4, 27, **45**, 51, **112**
tubers 39
tufted alpines 6, 18
tulips 24
tumbling Ted (*Saponaria ocymoides*) 7, 51, 90, 127
'Snow Tip' 127, **74**, 127

U
Ulmus

parvifolia
'Hokkaido' 24
unusual containers 76

V
Vaccinium 61
Veronica 4, 34, 86, 87, 137
austriaca
'Ionian Skies' 137
'Royal Blue' 93, 137
pectinata **7**, **47**, 59, 77, **137**
peduncularis
'Georgia Blue' 137
pinnata
'Blue Eyes' **62**, **137**
prostrata 16, 20, 24, 87, **94**, 137
'Blue Sheen' 61, **62**, 137
'Mrs Holt' **86**, 137
'Nana' **78**, 137
'Trehane' 137
spicata
'Alba' **97**
'Heidekind' 137
'Vestal' (*Anemone*) 101
'Video' (*Sempervivum*) 132
'Vindictive' (*Armeria*) 93, 103
vine weevils **38**
Viola (violet) 17, 90, 138
cornuta
'Alba Minor' 138
hederacea **138**
'Milkmaid' 138
'Molly Sanderson' 138
'Moonlight' 138
pedata (bird's foot violet) 138
verecunda 138
'Violet Queen' (*Phlox*) 24, 123

W
walls 90, 107, 116, 122
waterfalls 86

watering **32**, 34, 36, 49, 59, 85, 88, 89, 92
waterlogging 36–7, 86
waterproof covers 36
websites 41
weed control membrane 84
weedkillers 84
weeds 89
'Weihenstephaner Gold' (*Sedum*) 24, 92, 97, 131
'Weisser Zwerg' (*Iberis*) 116
'Whatfield Joy' (*Dianthus*) 24, **62**, 73, **108**
'Whatfield Magenta' (*Dianthus*) 108
'Whatfield Wisp' (*Dianthus*) 21, 24, **81**, 108
'Whitehill' (*Saxifraga*) 128
willowherb (*Epilobium*)
crassum 17, 51, 109
'Winifred Bevington' (*Saxifraga*) 22, 51, 128
'Wisley Flame' (*Penstemon*) **62**, 91, 122
'Wisley Primrose' (*Helianthemum*) 24, 114
wood amemone (*Anemone nemorosa*) 4, 101
'Robinsoniana' 101
'Vestal' 101
wood preservative 75
wooden containers **75–6**
wooden half-round rails **56**
woodland plantings 58
woodland plants 4
woods 4
Woodsia
polystichoides 24
woody plants 4

TITLES AVAILABLE FROM
GMC Publications
BOOKS

WOODCARVING

Beginning Woodcarving	GMC Publications
Carving Architectural Detail in Wood: The Classical Tradition	Frederick Wilbur
Carving Birds & Beasts	GMC Publications
Carving the Human Figure: Studies in Wood and Stone	Dick Onians
Carving Nature: Wildlife Studies in Wood	Frank Fox-Wilson
Carving on Turning	Chris Pye
Decorative Woodcarving	Jeremy Williams
Elements of Woodcarving	Chris Pye
Essential Woodcarving Techniques	Dick Onians
Lettercarving in Wood: A Practical Course	Chris Pye
Making & Using Working Drawings for Realistic Model Animals	
	Basil F. Fordham
Power Tools for Woodcarving	David Tippey
Relief Carving in Wood: A Practical Introduction	Chris Pye
Understanding Woodcarving in the Round	GMC Publications
Useful Techniques for Woodcarvers	GMC Publications
Woodcarving: A Foundation Course	Zoë Gertner
Woodcarving for Beginners	GMC Publications
Woodcarving Tools, Materials & Equipment (New Edition in 2 vols.)	
	Chris Pye

WOODTURNING

Adventures in Woodturning	David Springett
Bert Marsh: Woodturner	Bert Marsh
Bowl Turning Techniques Masterclass	Tony Boase
Chris Child's Projects for Woodturners	Chris Child
Colouring Techniques for Woodturners	Jan Sanders
Contemporary Turned Wood: New Perspectives in a Rich Tradition	
	Ray Leier, Jan Peters & Kevin Wallace
The Craftsman Woodturner	Peter Child
Decorating Turned Wood: The Maker's Eye	Liz & Michael O'Donnell
Decorative Techniques for Woodturners	Hilary Bowen
Illustrated Woodturning Techniques	John Hunnex
Intermediate Woodturning Projects	GMC Publications
Keith Rowley's Woodturning Projects	Keith Rowley
Making Screw Threads in Wood	Fred Holder
Turned Boxes: 50 Designs	Chris Stott
Turning Green Wood	Michael O'Donnell
Turning Pens and Pencils	Kip Christensen & Rex Burningham
Useful Woodturning Projects	GMC Publications
Woodturning: Bowls, Platters, Hollow Forms, Vases, Vessels, Bottles, Flasks, Tankards, Plates	GMC Publications
Woodturning: A Foundation Course (New Edition)	Keith Rowley
Woodturning: A Fresh Approach	Robert Chapman
Woodturning: An Individual Approach	Dave Regester
Woodturning: A Source Book of Shapes	John Hunnex
Woodturning Jewellery	Hilary Bowen
Woodturning Masterclass	Tony Boase
Woodturning Techniques	GMC Publications

CRAFTS

American Patchwork Designs in Needlepoint	Melanie Tacon
A Beginners' Guide to Rubber Stamping	Brenda Hunt
Beginning Picture Marquetry	Lawrence Threadgold
Blackwork: A New Approach	Brenda Day
Celtic Cross Stitch Designs	Carol Phillipson
Celtic Knotwork Designs	Sheila Sturrock
Celtic Knotwork Handbook	Sheila Sturrock
Celtic Spirals and Other Designs	Sheila Sturrock
Complete Pyrography	Stephen Poole
Creative Backstitch	Helen Hall
Creative Embroidery Techniques Using Colour Through Gold	
	Daphne J. Ashby & Jackie Woolsey
The Creative Quilter: Techniques and Projects	Pauline Brown
Cross-Stitch Designs from China	Carol Phillipson
Decoration on Fabric: A Sourcebook of Ideas	Pauline Brown
Decorative Beaded Purses	Enid Taylor
Designing and Making Cards	Glennis Gilruth
Glass Engraving Pattern Book	John Everett
Glass Painting	Emma Sedman
Handcrafted Rugs	Sandra Hardy
How to Arrange Flowers: A Japanese Approach to English Design	
	Taeko Marvelly
How to Make First-Class Cards	Debbie Brown
An Introduction to Crewel Embroidery	Mave Glenny
Making and Using Working Drawings for Realistic Model Animals	
	Basil F. Fordham
Making Character Bears	Valerie Tyler
Making Decorative Screens	Amanda Howes
Making Fabergé-Style Eggs	Denise Hopper
Making Fairies and Fantastical Creatures	Julie Sharp
Making Greetings Cards for Beginners	Pat Sutherland
Making Hand-Sewn Boxes: Techniques and Projects	Jackie Woolsey
Making Knitwear Fit	Pat Ashforth & Steve Plummer
Making Mini Cards, Gift Tags & Invitations	Glennis Gilruth
Making Soft-Bodied Dough Characters	Patricia Hughes
Natural Ideas for Christmas: Fantastic Decorations to Make	
	Josie Cameron-Ashcroft & Carol Cox
New Ideas for Crochet: Stylish Projects for the Home	Darsha Capaldi
Papercraft Projects for Special Occasions	Sine Chesterman
Patchwork for Beginners	Pauline Brown
Pyrography Designs	Norma Gregory
Pyrography Handbook (Practical Crafts)	Stephen Poole
Rose Windows for Quilters	Angela Besley
Rubber Stamping with Other Crafts	Lynne Garner
Sponge Painting	Ann Rooney
Stained Glass: Techniques and Projects	Mary Shanahan
Step-by-Step Pyrography Projects for the Solid Point Machine	Norma Gregory
Tassel Making for Beginners	Enid Taylor
Tatting Collage	Lindsay Rogers
Tatting Patterns	Lyn Morton
Temari: A Traditional Japanese Embroidery Technique	Margaret Ludlow

Trip Around the World: 25 Patchwork, Quilting and Appliqué Projects

        Gail Lawther

Trompe l'Oeil: Techniques and Projects   *Jan Lee Johnson*

Tudor Treasures to Embroider   *Pamela Warner*

Wax Art   *Hazel Marsh*

GARDENING

Auriculas for Everyone: How to Grow and Show Perfect Plants

        Mary Robinson

Beginners' Guide to Herb Gardening   *Yvonne Cuthbertson*

Beginners' Guide to Water Gardening   *Graham Clarke*

Bird Boxes and Feeders for the Garden   *Dave Mackenzie*

The Birdwatcher's Garden   *Hazel & Pamela Johnson*

Broad-Leaved Evergreens   *Stephen G. Haw*

Companions to Clematis: Growing Clematis with Other Plants

        Marigold Badcock

Creating Contrast with Dark Plants   *Freya Martin*

Creating Small Habitats for Wildlife in your Garden   *Josie Briggs*

Exotics are Easy   *GMC Publications*

Gardening with Hebes   *Chris & Valerie Wheeler*

Gardening with Wild Plants   *Julian Slatcher*

Growing Cacti and Other Succulents in the Conservatory and Indoors

        Shirley-Anne Bell

Growing Cacti and Other Succulents in the Garden   *Shirley-Anne Bell*

Hardy Perennials: A Beginner's Guide   *Eric Sawford*

Hedges: Creating Screens and Edges   *Averil Bedrich*

The Living Tropical Greenhouse: Creating a Haven for Butterflies

        John & Maureen Tampion

Marginal Plants   *Bernard Sleeman*

Orchids are Easy: A Beginner's Guide to their Care and Cultivation

        Tom Gilland

Plant Alert: A Garden Guide for Parents   *Catherine Collins*

Planting Plans for Your Garden   *Jenny Shukman*

Plants that Span the Seasons   *Roger Wilson*

Sink and Container Gardening Using Dwarf Hardy Plants

        Chris & Valerie Wheeler

The Successful Conservatory and Growing Exotic Plants   *Joan Phelan*

Tropical Garden Style with Hardy Plants   *Alan Hemsley*

Water Garden Projects: From Groundwork to Planting   *Roger Sweetinburgh*

PHOTOGRAPHY

Close-Up on Insects   *Robert Thompson*

An Essential Guide to Bird Photography   *Steve Young*

Field Guide to Landscape Photography   *Peter Watson*

How to Photograph your Pet   *Nick Ridley*

Light in the Landscape: A Photographer's Year   *Peter Watson*

Outdoor Photography Portfolio   *GMC Publications*

Photographing Fungi in the Field   *George McCarthy*

Photography for the Naturalist   *Mark Lucock*

Viewpoints from *Outdoor Photography*   *GMC Publications*

Where and How to Photograph Wildlife   *Peter Evans*

Wild Life: A Photographer's Year   *Andy Rouse*

ART TECHNIQUES

Oil Paintings from your Garden: A Guide for Beginners   *Rachel Shirley*

MAGAZINES

WOODTURNING ◆ WOODCARVING ◆ FURNITURE & CABINETMAKING

THE ROUTER ◆ WOODWORKING ◆ THE DOLLS' HOUSE MAGAZINE

OUTDOOR PHOTOGRAPHY ◆ BLACK & WHITE PHOTOGRAPHY

TRAVEL PHOTOGRAPHY

MACHINE KNITTING NEWS ◆ BUSINESSMATTERS

The above represents a full list of all titles currently published or scheduled to be published.
All are available direct from the Publishers or through bookshops, newsagents and specialist retailers.
To place an order, or to obtain a complete catalogue, contact:

GMC Publications,
Castle Place, 166 High Street, Lewes, East Sussex BN7 1XU, United Kingdom
Tel: 01273 488005 Fax: 01273 478606
E-mail: pubs@thegmcgroup.com

Orders by credit card are accepted

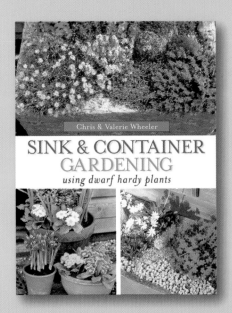
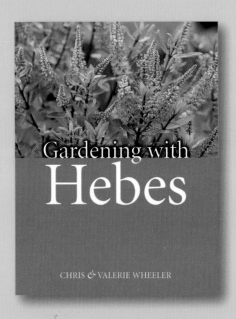